The Greatest Power in the World

The Greatest Power in the World

Kathryn Kuhlman

Bridge-Logos *Publishers*

North Brunswick, NJ

Unless otherwise stated, all Scripture quotes are taken from the King James Version of the Bible.

The Greatest Power in the World
by Kathryn Kuhlman
ISBN: 0-88270-740-X
Library of Congress Catalog Card Number: 97-73696
Copyright © 1997 by The Kathryn Kuhlman Foundation

Published by:
Bridge-Logos *Publishers*
North Brunswick Corporate Center
1300 Airport Road, Suite E
North Brunswick, NJ 08902

Contents

The Seal of the Holy Spirit

Foreword

The sermons and heart-to-heart radio talks by Kathryn Kuhlman, which were a source of blessing to literally thousands during her lifetime, are as relevant in today's world as when she stood before her congregations or sat before the microphone in her radio studio delivering God's precious Word.

Since Kathryn Kuhlman went Home to be with the Lord on February 20, 1976, the Foundation has received countless requests for her messages on the Holy Spirit. Because there is such a hunger in the hearts of men and women today to know more about this mighty Third Person of the Trinity, and to experience His power in and through their lives, we have gathered together some of the messages to share with you in this book.

She often said, "Any results there might be in this life of mine, is not Kathryn Kuhlman. It's the Holy Spirit; it's what the Holy Spirit does through a yielded vessel," and "The Holy Spirit will magnify and glorify only one person and that one person is Jesus Christ, the Son of the Living God."

Beloved, if you are a Christian, an heir of God and a joint-heir with Christ Jesus, then that glorious experience of being filled with the Holy Spirit is for you. It is a part of your inheritance.

We pray as you read these messages, you will not only be blessed, but challenged—for there is much *more* in Jesus Christ, and so *much more* in the power of God than you or I can realize. He will take that which we surrender and fill it with the Holy Spirit. If you have not made that full surrender to Jesus, do it now! God bless you!

The Kathryn Kuhlman Foundation

The Holy Spirit in the Old Testament

1

The Holy Spirit: In Existence Always

*Y*ou will agree, I am sure, that thousands of professing Christians of all denominations give honor to the Holy Spirit each Lord's Day morning as they sing the Doxology. Both Catholics and Protestants fill our churches, singing the Doxology or speaking the name of the Holy Spirit; yet, very few know anything about Him or even believe in Him as a person. We think we know about God the Father, regarding

Him as the great Creator. We understand Jesus, the Son of the Living God, who came and walked upon the earth, and died on the Cross. He is no mystery to thousands of people; but when it comes to the Holy Spirit, practically little or nothing is known about Him.

Therefore, in laying the ground work for this series about the Holy Spirit, I want you to know that when I speak of the Day of Pentecost, I am talking about the time when the Word was fulfilled, even as Jesus promised before He went away (John 16:7). He said that it was expedient that He go away because He was to assume the position of great High Priest, seated on the right hand of God the Father. He could not stay here, but He said He would not leave us comfortless or without power. He promised us power in our own personal lives and also that He would give power to the Church through the person of the Holy Spirit. Jesus said that this mighty Third Person of the Trinity would come after He had gone back to the Father; and, at that time, Jesus would fill His new position of great High Priest. The Holy Spirit also would assume a new position, one that He had never filled before.

Now in speaking of the Day of Pentecost, I am not talking about only one experience that they had in the Upper Room when the Holy Spirit came. We are living in the Day of Pentecost, and this Day of Pentecost will continue until that moment when the Holy Spirit leaves this earth even as Jesus left. And when He leaves, the Holy Spirit will take with Him the Church made up of believers who have been born into the Body of Christ.

What we are going to discuss here is the person of the Holy Spirit and His work prior to the Day of Pentecost, so that you may become better acquainted with the person of the Holy Spirit who has been in existence always. This may be quite an eye opener if you have thought of Him as a personality existing only since the Day of Pentecost. He

4

was present at the time of creation; we see this as we read Genesis 1:1-2: "In the beginning God created the heaven and the earth. And the earth was without form, and void; and darkness was upon the face of the deep. And the Spirit of God moved upon the face of the waters."

I shall never forget the moment the Holy Spirit revealed a very marvelous truth to my heart. I feel it was one of the greatest revelations I've ever received when He made it clear to me that the entire Bible from Genesis through the last book of the New Testament, the Book of the Revelation, is a revelation of one person: Jesus, the Son of God. The Bible is the Word of God, its author is the Holy Spirit, and in its entirety it is the revelation of Jesus Christ.

Now I am sure you are familiar with the account of Eve's temptation in the Garden of Eden, the sin of both Adam and Eve, and that they were driven by God from the garden lest they eat of the tree of life and live forever in their fallen state (Genesis 3:22-24).

God is never defeated, however, and I believe this prompted God to call for a conference in heaven where the three Persons of the Godhead met—the Father, the Son, and the Holy Spirit—to discuss the sacrifice that must be provided for man's redemption. Around that conference table these three gathered, each with a distinct personality, but always working in perfect harmony and in conjunction one with the other. It was there at that conference that a plan was devised for man's redemption. They knew that the price must be paid by one that sin had never touched, a pure and sinless man, and Jesus turned to the Father and offered Himself, through the Holy Spirit, to be given for man's salvation. We often quote John 3:16, one of the best known Bible verses; but, beloved, God could not have given His only begotten Son if His Son had not first of all been willing to come to earth as a sacrifice. No, the Father could not have given Jesus as that wonderful gift of love to humanity, except Jesus had first of all offered Himself as a sacrifice.

As a result, Jesus agreed to take upon Himself the form of man and to pay the price for man's salvation. It is the blood that makes an atonement for the soul (Leviticus 17:11); but, only sinless blood, blood that sin had never touched, blood of one who had never known sin, could meet that condition and pay that price. There was only one who could meet this criterion: God's perfect Son.

Try to envision that meeting where the three conferred. I believe the Holy Spirit, who is the power of the Trinity, must have turned to Jesus and vowed, "I will do my part in fulfilling the plan. If you go, I will take care of your 'press,' I will be your promotion man."

Please do not think me sacrilegious when I say these words. I mean them with all of my heart in a very sacred way. I believe that the Holy Spirit meant: "If you go to earth and give your life as a sacrifice for lost humanity, the least I can do is promote you and reveal your love and purpose to the hearts of men and women." And from that moment, the Holy Spirit began His marvelous promotion of Jesus, glorifying Jesus' name and pointing to the Christ. He did not wait until Jesus came in the form of a babe that first Christmas morning. He began to reveal Jesus to the hearts of men and women immediately.

Let me remind you that whenever the words "the Spirit of God" are used in the Bible, they always refer to the Holy Spirit. They do not refer to God the Father, neither do they refer to Jesus Christ the Son. Whether in the Old or the New Testament, the words "the Spirit of God" refer to the Holy Spirit.

It was the same Holy Spirit who gave the Old Testament and New Testament prophets all of the revelations that they received. It was the Holy Spirit who revealed to John all that is recorded in the last book of the New

Testament. At the very outset of Revelation, John says: "I was in the Spirit on the Lord's day" (Revelation 1:10). All that John received in prophecy regarding these last days, we are seeing literally fulfilled before our very eyes. That which was prophesied and looked for with expectation for generations is now quickly becoming history. The most up-to-date book that we have today is the last book of the New Testament—*The Revelation of Jesus Christ.*

All these things were given by revelation of the Holy Spirit in exactly the same way the Holy Spirit gave revelations to the Old Testament prophets. The Holy Spirit gave those revelations to Jeremiah, to Isaiah, and to all the Old Testament prophets. The things they prophesied did not come by their own understanding, and that is the reason there are no contradictions in either the Old Testament or the New Testament. The same person, the Holy Spirit, was the one who gave all revelations.

Within this precious Word of God, the Holy Spirit has revealed all the truth that is necessary for us to know concerning the things of God. Upon these truths, a person may build for time and eternity. It is God's revelation given by inspiration of the Holy Spirit. The Book of Hebrews affirms that God's Word is a living power, sharper than any two-edged sword, that can pierce to the depths of the soul and spirit (Hebrews 4:12). And if the Word of God was given by inspiration of God by the Holy Spirit—and it was—then we must listen to it, we must believe it, and we must obey it.

Long before the Holy Spirit came on the Day of Pentecost, long before the Holy Spirit made His appearance to those believers in the Upper Room, He was active in revelation—for all the prophets received their inspiration and their revelations from the Third Person of the Trinity. Now let's leave the *general ministry* of the Holy Spirit and study His ministry to individuals who lived in Old Testament days.

As we do, let's remember that the most important thing in the world to God is the individual person. *You* are important to Him. There is nothing that is more thrilling to me than to see how He works in the life of an individual—to watch Him take an earthen vessel, a surrendered life, and see the Holy Spirit work in and through that life. There is no greater compliment than to have the Holy Spirit work in and through the life of an individual.

2

One Spirit, One Purpose

*F*irst of all, let's look briefly into the life of Joseph. Pharaoh, who ruled over Egypt, recognized the power of the Holy Spirit in the life of this young man. Pharaoh knew, and you will also readily agree, that there was something different, something unusual, about Joseph's life. In the natural I don't believe Joseph differed greatly from any other man living then or today. But watch it. What made him unusual? What was the source of the power in the life of Joseph? Pharaoh recognized it and the account is given in Genesis 41:38: "Can we find such a one as this is, a man in whom the Spirit of God is?"

I wonder if Pharaoh really knew of whom he was speaking, and if he knew anything about the Third Person of the Trinity. One thing I am dead sure of, however, is that Pharaoh recognized the wisdom, knowledge, and supernatural power in the life of Joseph—a power greater than any human power—and he labeled it correctly. It was the Spirit of God in Joseph's life.

Now, in the thirty-first chapter of the Book of Exodus we will see something else that may be most enlightening. It concerns the workmen who erected the tabernacle in the wilderness. If you're a Bible student, you will recognize and readily agree that one of the most perfect works of art was the tabernacle in the wilderness. So far as craftsmanship and workmanship are concerned, it was absolutely perfect. Even architects in today's world have marveled at the skills and abilities of these men who worked on the tabernacle in the wilderness.

This is what God's Word states concerning these men: "I have filled him [Bazaleel, the head artisan] with the spirit of God, in wisdom, and in understanding, and in knowledge, and in all manner of workmanship, To devise cunning works, to work in gold, and in silver, and in brass, And in cutting of stones, to set them, and in carving of timber, to work in all manner of workmanship" (Exodus 31:3-5).

The Holy Spirit worked through these men. I dare say they were ordinary men with no unusual ability; but God, through the Holy Spirit, took their minds, took their hands, and they became absolute perfection in their skills. The tabernacle was to be erected according to a divine plan, with no imperfections whatsoever in its design or in the craftsmanship by which it was built. It was to be a perfect work in order that there should be a perfect temple in which God could dwell. The secret to its perfection was found in the Holy Spirit.

Here is something else that is most enlightening— it's in the eleventh chapter of the Book of Numbers. We all know that the Holy Spirit was upon Moses who, in the natural, was an ordinary man, a man with like passions as any man living today. Yet, he was one of the greatest leaders that the nation of Israel ever had.

What was the secret of the power in his life? What was the secret of his great leadership? It was the power of the Holy Spirit.

Even though he was a great leader, Moses had to have help, and God knew it; but counselors and advisors would only be a hindrance unless they, too, were of the same mind and had the same purpose. Therefore, it was necessary that the same Spirit—the Holy Spirit that indwelt Moses—also indwell those seventy men who surrounded Moses. So God took of the Spirit that was upon Moses and put it upon them. As a result, these seventy men, who now possessed a oneness in purpose, a oneness of mind and of Spirit in God, were set apart to become counselors and assistants and advisors in the responsibility of supervising the nation of Israel.

It is most difficult for a Spirit-filled person to work in perfect harmony and oneness of purpose with someone who is not Spirit-filled. I have found that there are some people that I would find impossible to work with day in and day out in the Lord's work. They would be no help to me whatsoever, although they are born-again Christians. You see, there is a difference when the Holy Spirit has taken over the life of an individual, has taken his mind, his body, fills him completely, and has given him the mind of Christ (1 Corinthians 2:16). It is then that it is not two or three minds, not several minds, but all minds working as one because it is the mind of Christ (1 Corinthians 1:10).

11

See how wonderfully God worked out this plan with Moses. There were seventy men who were set apart to help Moses in the responsibility of supervising the nation of Israel, and God said. "I will come down and talk with thee there: and I will take of the spirit which is upon thee, and will put it upon them; and they shall bear the burden of the people with thee, that thou bear it not thyself alone" (Numbers 11:17).

As far as I can determine, the Scriptures had not previously said that Moses was indwelt and empowered and made wise by the Spirit of God, but we can see the definite results of the Holy Spirit in the life and the leadership of Moses. God said in this passage that He would take the Spirit that was given to Moses and would give it to these seventy men. And that is exactly what He did: "And the Lord came down in a cloud, and spake unto him, and took of the spirit that was upon him, and gave it unto the seventy elders" (Numbers 11:25). Moses himself ministered by the gift of the Spirit that was given to him, and the seventy men who were his helpers also ministered by the gift of the Holy Spirit.

3

The Secret of Power

Gideon

*L*et us go to the Book of Judges now and there we will see the account of a man named Gideon. Do you want to know the secret of Gideon's power? It was the same Person who is the subject of this book: the Holy Spirit.

In Judges 6:34 the Scripture says, "The Spirit of the Lord came upon Gideon." And as we read on, we see the preparation of Gideon for the battle in which he and three hundred men were victorious. The significant thing, however, is that Gideon ministered because the Spirit of the Lord came upon him.

Samson

Now we come to another account, one about Samson as recorded in Judges 14:6: "The Spirit of the Lord came mightily upon him, and he rent him [the lion] as he would have rent a kid, and he had nothing in his hand."

We also read concerning Samson that the Philistines "shouted against him: and the Spirit of the Lord came mightily upon him, and the cords that were upon his arms became as flax that was burnt with fire" (Judges 15:14).

I remember that as a little girl I could have that story of Samson told to me over and over again. Oh, he was a wonderful giant of a man in my sight! The children of this generation may have their eyes on Batman or Superman, but when I was a youngster, my ideal was Samson, the strongest man that ever lived. He was my Superman, and many a child going to Sunday School felt the same way.

But do you want to know something? It was not until much later that I learned the secret of Samson's power. As a child, I thought it was because he let his hair grow, and I used to look at all long-haired men and think that they must be strong too, like Samson.

Studying the Word of God, however, I found that the secret of Samson's power and strength was not in his hair but in the Holy Spirit. Here was one raised up by God, upon whom the Spirit of God came, not once, but on a great number of occasions when there was need for a manifestation of divine power. It was not Samson's power. Nor was his power in the length of his hair. The length of his hair was only obedience to God. It was the Spirit of

God that came upon Samson so that he might do mighty feats by the power that was given to him.

The first step downward is always when one refuses to obey the Lord. Remember, the power in the life of Samson that enabled him to do what he did, was the power of the Holy Spirit. When Samson obeyed God, the Holy Spirit came upon him. But when he turned from obeying God, the mighty power of the Holy Spirit was taken from him. One of the saddest portions of God's Word is found in Judges 16:20: "And he awoke out of his sleep, and said, I will go out as at other times before, and shake myself. And he wist not that the Lord was departed from him."

Up until that time, beloved, it was the Holy Spirit who did the shaking as He came upon Samson. It was the Spirit of the Lord mightily upon Samson that made the cords that were upon his arms as flax that were burned with fire. But now, Samson was disobedient. He had grieved God and the Holy Spirit. Since it was the power of the Holy Spirit that had done the shaking before, there was a difference now. It is marvelous and wonderful when the Holy Spirit does the shaking. But here Samson was not aware of the fact that the Holy Spirit had departed from him, and now he had to shake himself. One is of the Spirit, one is of the flesh. The Holy Spirit had left Samson, and he became like any other man.

4

The Holy Spirit in the Life of Saul and David

*W*e have already seen the results of the power of the Holy Spirit as He came upon a few selected individuals during the Old Testament era. He gave special powers to some in their craftsmanship. With others, He used their tongue to speak, giving them the ability to lead or guide. To Samson He gave physical strength. But all were a sovereign act of God.

Today, as part of our inheritance as born-again men and women, we have the promise from the Master Himself of the indwelling of the Holy Spirit. It is God's plan and purpose that all who are born again should be filled with the Spirit; but it was not so in Old Testament times. Neither Moses, nor Joseph, nor Gideon, nor Samson were *filled with the Spirit* because of some special thing *within themselves*. They did not do something to merit the Holy Spirit's presence.

God gave them that gift sovereignly. They had nothing to do with it, nor could they receive the gift by asking for it. God chose them and made them His instruments. And the first important distinction to observe then is that the Holy Spirit's indwelling in the Old Testament was not universal for all believers. *But it is today, in this the Day of Pentecost.*

The second thing that we must observe is that the Holy Spirit came upon men to empower them for some special service. With Moses and the seventy it was to lead. With the workmen in the wilderness it was to construct the tabernacle that would be a habitation of God. It was God's design and it had to be perfect in construction and plan. Therefore, He gave power to these workmen and craftsmen, instructing them with supernatural intelligence to create a perfect building for Him to dwell therein. The ministry of the Holy Spirit was not to produce fellowship, not for acts of worship or praise, nor to bring those who were indwelt into a special relationship with God the Father or with the Son. The Holy Spirit was given to perform some special and definite work.

We are all familiar with the account of Saul who was anointed King of Israel and empowered whenever the Holy Spirit came upon him. But we read that "the Spirit of the Lord departed from Saul, and an evil spirit from the Lord troubled him" (1 Samuel 16:14). Here was a man who had wrought mighty deeds by the power of the Spirit, but now, because of the temporary nature of the Spirit's indwelling presence, the Spirit departed and Saul was left without His presence and power. The presence of the Holy Spirit was not something that was permanent with Saul. He came upon him only at intervals.

There is something, however, that has touched my own heart very deeply; and I believe that this is one exception to that which I have been saying. It concerns David. I have often wondered why David had such a special place in the heart of God, and I think it was because God knew David's heart. Psalm fifty-one reveals the real heart of David. He was sorry for his sin with Bathsheba.

His sin could not be hidden from the nation over which he ruled. It was in the open and could not be denied. Here was a man with whom the Spirit had come to abide, but David knew full well that his relationship to the Holy Spirit was not guaranteed to be a permanent thing. David was aware that because of his transgressions, the Spirit might leave him and cast him aside as God had cast aside Samson and Saul. David knew that as surely as the Spirit had been taken from Samson, as surely as the Spirit had left Saul, the Spirit could also leave him. So David asked God, on the basis of His mercy, to purge him from his sin, and to apply the blood of sacrifice and the water of cleansing.

Oh, if you want to see the sincerity of David's heart, if you want to see the real David, you will see it as he cried out in the fifty-first Psalm, "Have mercy upon me, O God, according to thy lovingkindness: according unto the multitude of thy tender mercies blot out my transgressions" (Psalm 51:1). [50]

There are men and women today who were once used of God who will not acknowledge their sins. If you are one of these people, your starting point right now is to come to the place where you acknowledge your transgressions and your sins before God.

David said, "Against thee, thee only, have I sinned, and done this evil in thy sight: that thou mightest be justified when thou speakest, and be clear when thou judgest. Behold, I was shapen in iniquity; and in sin did my mother conceive me. Behold, thou desirest truth in the inward parts: and in the hidden part thou shalt make me to know wisdom. Purge me with hyssop, and I shall be clean: wash me, and I shall be whiter than snow. Make me to hear joy and gladness; that the bones which thou hast broken may rejoice. Hide thy face from my sins, and blot out all mine iniquities. Create in me a clean heart, O God; and renew a right spirit within me" (Psalm 51:4-10).

Then comes the cry from the very depths of the heart of a man who is repenting for his sin. We see here a cry of real repentance, and at the same time a glimpse into the greatest fear that David ever knew. It is stated in the next seven words of that Psalm, verse 11: "Take not thy Holy Spirit from me." David knew that the Holy Spirit had been taken from Saul. He knew the Holy Spirit had been taken from Samson, and that Samson "wist not that the Lord was departed from him." So David, fearing lest the same marvelous power and Spirit be taken from him, cried out: "Cast me not away from thy presence; and take not thy holy spirit from me."

In other words, David was saying: "Take everything else that I might have; take any earthly possessions that may be mine; take any earthly power that I might possess. Take it all, but please cast me not away from Thy Presence, O God; and take not Thy Holy Spirit from me. For when He is departed, I am just mere flesh, an ordinary man without power."

5

The Holy Spirit: The Same Then and Now

*I*t is evident that the outpouring of the Holy Spirit during the Old Testament was a sovereign act of God. Without fear of contradiction, I say that all the prophets of the Old Testament spoke as truth was revealed to them by the Holy Spirit. The Scripture in 1 Corinthians 2:10-11 confirms my statement: "God hath revealed them [the things that God prepared] unto us by his

Spirit: for the Spirit searcheth all things, yea, the deep things of God. For what man knoweth the things of a man, save the spirit of man which is in him? even so the things of God knoweth no man, but the Spirit of God."

All revelation is given by the Holy Spirit, and when man receives the knowledge of that revelation, that too is given by the same mighty Third Person of the Trinity. I marvel sometimes at that precious little old godly mother, a dear saint of God, who, when it comes to most things, is illiterate. Yet, she can know more about the Bible, and about spiritual things than somebody who has all his degrees. Somebody who may be admired and looked up to and esteemed because of his great learning, but to whom the Bible holds no real truths and who has practically no understanding of God's Word whatsoever. Why would a godly mother know more about the Bible than a Bible scholar? Because the Bible is a spiritual book, and it must be spiritually revealed by the Holy Spirit, even as He has been its inspiration.

Education is wonderful, and please do not say that I am decrying education. What I am saying is this: The Bible is different from law, medicine, or any other teaching in the whole world. The Holy Spirit is its inspiration. The Scriptures have been given by the Holy Spirit. They can only be revealed to the hearts and minds of men and women through the Holy Spirit, and this is something that you cannot go to school to obtain. You receive the Holy Spirit on your knees and His revelations must come straight from Him.

Here is a Book, the Holy Bible, and it dares to write out in advance the future history of this world. It dares to prophesy what is actually going to happen to the nations of the world. Here is a Book that literally dares to tell the future of mankind, and a fool is the person who will take issue with the Word of God because everything that has been prophesied, regarding the events to happen up until this very hour, has taken place.

Read the Old Testament. In the life of Jesus Christ the Son of God, dozens of prophecies were fulfilled; but the Old Testament prophets had never seen Jesus. They were only moved upon by the Holy Spirit to give the predictions and the prophecies. In the New Testament we see in Acts 1:16 that the revelation of truth is found in the person of the Holy Spirit. The disciples were gathered in the Upper Room and Peter said, "Men and brethren, this scripture must needs have been fulfilled, which the Holy Ghost by the mouth of David spake before concerning Judas." Here Peter was making reference to Psalm 41:9 regarding the betrayal of Jesus: "Yea, mine own familiar friend, in whom I trusted, which did eat of my bread, hath lifted up his heel against me."

If you do not think that the Bible is the most supernatural book, if you do not think that the Bible is the most up-to-date book ever written, if you think that it is out-moded and out-dated, my friend, you have another think coming. Blow the dust off your Bible. Start reading it. It is dynamite, and God is going to keep His Word to the crossing of every "t" and the dotting of every "i." Again I remind you: if I teach you one thing and the Bible says another, the Bible is right. You can stake your very life on the Bible. Don't ever take issue with the Bible. It's a supernatural book, supernaturally inspired. One speaks in error if he should say that there are contradictions in the Word of God. There are no contradictions in the New Testament concerning that which is in the Old, and there are no contradictions in the Old Testament concerning that which is in the New. They were both given under the same inspiration of the Holy Spirit and He does not contradict Himself.

Here is something that is marvelous, and I quote Peter: "Knowing this first, that no prophecy of the scripture is of any private interpretation. For the prophecy came not in old time by the will of man: but holy men of God spake as they were moved by the Holy Ghost" (2 Peter 1:20-21).

What does that mean? Simply that prophecy did not originate in the mind of the author who did the writing. The one who did the writing only supplied the vessel, the body, the flesh, as a stenographer. Even as today the Holy Spirit asks only for a yielded vessel, and it is His power that works through the empty, yielded vessel.

The Holy Spirit in the New Testament

6

The Holy Spirit Reveals Jesus

*T*he Old and the New Testaments of the Bible are not two separate books. They are one book, and no person can fully understand one without the other. My next statement may be one you have never considered before but it is vitally important. *The Bible has only one author.* I am fully aware that approximately forty men were used by the Holy Spirit to write the many books of the Bible. I am not sure what we should label these men, but whatever term we might employ, we know in the final analysis that the Holy Spirit is the author of the Word of God. That explains why there are no contradictions between the Old Testament and the New Testament. The Holy Spirit was and is the only author of the Word of God, for the Bible plainly states that "prophecy came not in old time by the will of man; but holy men of God spake as they were moved by the Holy Ghost" (2 Peter 1:21).

The Apostle Paul never met David because they lived in different generations and in separate dispensations. Neither did Paul live in the era of Jeremiah or Isaiah; yet that which all these men wrote, and that which they spoke, was in perfect harmony and accord one with the other. Why? Because it was the same Holy Spirit who worked through each of these men.

Consider something with me. The Passover was instituted the night that God led the children of Israel out of Egypt. God delivered the children of Israel from the hand of Pharaoh and set them free from Egyptian bondage as a result of the tenth plague. As a means of identification to the death angel, the Israelites were commanded to place the blood of a sacrificial lamb on the side posts and top of their doors. God promised that when the death angel saw the covering of the blood of a spotless lamb over and around the door, it would be a sign to him to "pass over" that home and death would not strike there. And from that time forward, the Passover was observed every year as a memorial to God's great deliverance and God's protection.

Now go to the New Testament. In Paul's first epistle to the Corinthian believers, he speaks of Christ who is our Passover Lamb, sacrificed for us. As we place Leviticus alongside of the New Testament, we can see that that which took place in the Old Testament was in anticipation of an event in the New Testament. The Lord Jesus Christ, as the

Son of God, shed His blood that we might come under the covering of His blood, and that He might hover over us to protect us as His own. Jesus is the Lamb of God that takes away the sin of the world; and by the sprinkling of the blood of the lamb without spot and blemish at that Passover in Egypt, we see a type and a shadow of the One who was to come in the future—the very Son of the Living God. Now, we who are Christians, commemorate the Passover celebration every time we receive communion and partake of the broken bread and the wine at the Lord's Supper.

Let us go a little farther to the Feast of Unleavened Bread, a very sacred feast that follows the Passover and is still observed by Orthodox Jews. Those who observed the Passover and feasted on the Passover lamb were to observe a seven-day period in which there was no leaven in their homes. Leaven is the sign of uncleanness.

Turn with me now to the New Testament again, to what Paul writes to the Church in Corinth. Believers were exhorted to purge out therefore the old leaven (1 Corinthians 5:7). What does it mean? Simply that the one who has been born again has been cleansed by the blood of the Lamb, and is therefore a new creature in Christ Jesus. The blood of Christ not only makes an atonement for the soul, but the blood cleanses. Paul said, "Purge out therefore the old leaven," and as we are new creatures in Christ Jesus after we have been born again, we have a new kind of life. "Old things are passed away; behold, all things are become new" (2 Corinthians 5:17). There is now a communion with Christ and a holy walk with Him.

The third feast described in the Old Testament is the Feast of Firstfruits. The children of Israel were to bring a sheaf of the firstfruits of that harvest to the priest that he might wave the sheaf as an offering before the Lord (Leviticus 23:10-14). In the New Testament, this feast is typical of resurrection, first of Christ and then "afterward they that are Christ's at his coming" (1 Corinthians 15:23). Read the whole 15th chapter of this epistle, but especially this 23rd verse in connection with what I am saying.

Christ is the firstfruits of those who will follow Him in the harvest. Because of His resurrection and because He lives, we too shall live. We need have no fear or worry, no anxiety regarding the resurrection of our body. We need have no fear of death. Why? Because He is the firstfruits. He has gone before us. No tomb could hold His body. He lives. He is at the Father's right hand. He is the firstfruits and one day we shall be like Him.

You will notice that God has instituted these feasts according to a prearranged plan. Christ, who is our Passover, redeems by blood and brings those who are saved into a new kind of life. Christ, who is the wave sheaf, is the firstfruits of the harvest that will be brought to God by His resurrection. So here in the Old Testament you have Christ crucified and Christ resurrected, as represented in these two feasts.

The Feast of Pentecost is next, following fifty days after the Feast of Firstfruits. Moses was told "ye shall number fifty days and ye shall offer a new meat-offering unto the Lord. Ye shall bring out of your habitations two wave-loaves" (Leviticus 23:16-17). The children of Israel who had passed through the harvest of the firstfruits were to take the wheat of that harvest, grind it into flour, bake the flour into bread, and then offer that bread to God. The offering on the second thanksgiving service was not one of sheaves, but rather of loaves, that which had been unified, put together, and then offered to God.

See something now. Jesus is our Passover Lamb who has been sacrificed for us. There will be a new life in Him, a life without leaven. When we are born again and because we belong to Him by His resurrection, He promises us a resurrection like unto His. Then we shall be like Him in our resurrected bodies. We shall see Him face to face.

Now watch. When we come to this Feast of Pentecost, we are moving into the realm of the Holy Spirit, for He is the agent who will unite the people and present the Church unto God: perfect and unified. That is exactly what the Holy Spirit is doing today. We are no longer individual sheaves, but a loaf today—His church. When we accept Christ in the forgiveness of our sins, we are born into this Body that is called the Church. It makes no difference whether we are Jew or Gentile, whether we are Catholic or Protestant; it makes no difference where we have our church membership or what may be our nationality. The thing that makes all the difference in the world is this experience of being born again, that we have accepted the very Son of the Living God in the forgiveness of our sins. It is the blood that makes an atonement for the soul. Not just any blood, but Christ's blood, for He is absolute perfection, sin never having touched His body. His is the only blood that was pure blood, the blood of the Son of the Living God.

The Holy Spirit has a very definite work in this dispensation in which we live: the formation of the Body of Christ, His Church. At Pentecost, the Holy Spirit took up residence on earth and He will remain here until the Church is complete. Watch His mighty office work now! You will remember that I told you that Jesus offered Himself through the Holy Spirit to be given for mankind's sacrifice, and that the Holy Spirit promised to be Christ's agent. He vowed to promote and lift up Jesus, and that is why, when Jesus was still here on earth, He spoke of the Holy Spirit who was soon to come.

You will find His conversation in the 16th Chapter of the Gospel of John: "But now I go my way to him that sent me" (John 16:5). Of whom is Jesus speaking? It was God the Father who had sent Him. He goes on, "Nevertheless I tell you the truth; It is expedient for you that I go away" (verse 7). Here Jesus explains to His disciples why it was necessary that He go away—so He could fulfill the Father's perfect plan. The time was nearing when He must return to the Father and assume the position of great High Priest. But He promised He would not leave them alone or comfortless. There would be one, the Holy Spirit, who would come and carry out a most important work—the forming of that "loaf" that was represented at the Feast of Pentecost that followed fifty days after the Passover.

> *For if I go not away, the Comforter will not come unto you; but if I depart, I will send him unto you.*
>
> *And when he is come, he will reprove the world of sin [there is conviction], and of righteousness, and of judgment.*
>
> *Of sin, because they believe not on me;*
>
> *Of righteousness, because I go to my Father, and ye see me no more;*
>
> *Of judgment, because the prince of this world is judged.*
>
> *I have yet many things to say unto you, but ye cannot bear them now.*
>
> (John 16:7-12)

Jesus knew His disciples would not fully understand all that He was saying to them, but He knew that shortly the Holy Spirit would come and take up His residence here on earth with them and carry out His assignment. *The Holy Spirit came, and He is still here!*

> *Howbeit when he, the Spirit of truth, is come, he will guide you into all truth: for he shall not speak of*

himself; but whatsoever he shall hear, that shall he speak: and he will show you things to come.

He shall glorify me. . . .

(John 16:13-14)

What did I tell you earlier? The Holy Spirit always glorifies Jesus, always promotes Jesus. The Holy Spirit is Jesus' agent. Throughout the entire Bible, He speaks of Jesus, reveals Jesus, and Jesus here says, "He will glorify me: for he shall receive of mine, and shall shew it unto you. All things that the Father hath are mine: therefore said I, that he shall take of mine, and shall shew it unto you" (John 16:14-15).

Thus we clearly see that no person can know the Holy Spirit, whether in the Old Testament or the New Testament, without knowing Jesus; for the Holy Spirit always magnifies and reveals Jesus Christ, God's Son. *And He continues to fulfill His mission to this very hour!*

7

The Reality of the Holy Spirit

*N*ow if you don't like cornbread, maybe you'll like the kind of cornbread that I'm bringing you. It's a little different from the usual kind. It's old-fashioned, it's good for you, and it will feed your soul with good spiritual food. It's about the reality of the Holy Spirit.

Let me share with you a Scripture that I pray shall be most enlightening to you. It's found in the 9th chapter of

Hebrews, the 14th verse: "How much more shall the blood of Christ, who through the eternal Spirit [and remember that the eternal Spirit is the Holy Spirit] offered himself without spot to God."

Now, there are few youngsters who have ever attended Sunday School or even professing Christians of any age who do not know John 3:16. Whether they know any other Scripture, they know the one that says, "For God so loved the world, that he gave his only begotten Son." You will recall that in an earlier chapter, we considered something that had to happen before God gave Jesus as an offering for our sins. He could not have given Jesus if Jesus had not first of all given Himself, and the Scripture that we read in Hebrews says that Jesus offered Himself to God the Father through the Holy Spirit.

Why? Because Jesus knew that in giving Himself, He would have to take the form of a man. He would be conceived of the Holy Spirit in the womb of a woman, and in walking upon the earth, He would be as much man as though He were not God. He knew everything that would be involved when He offered Himself. He knew that one day He would stand face to face with Satan, with the devil himself. He knew Satan's strength and power. He also knew the weakness of man, for man had fallen. He knew that in the form of man walking the shores of Galilee, He would face satanic power, be confronted with temptations that all of us face as human beings. He also knew that in the form of human flesh He would be able to yield to those temptations.

I pause here just a minute for there are some who try to tell us that Jesus Christ could not have yielded to temptation when Satan came and tempted Him in the wilderness. If Jesus could not have yielded, then His temptations would have been a farce. Before He offered Himself through the Holy Spirit for man's redemption, He

36

had perfect knowledge that in coming to this earth He was coming on Satan's territory. Jesus did not hold the title deed to this earth when He came in the form of flesh, and both Jesus and Satan knew that.

Yes, Jesus knew full well He was coming on the devil's territory, but He also knew He would have to have the Holy Spirit as His wonderful Strengthener in order to withstand the temptations of Satan. He knew that to convince skeptical men and women, there would have to be proof of His divinity. He knew there would have to be miracles, works of power, that men and women could see with their eyes. But coming in the form of man, as much man as though He were not deity, He knew He could not do these things in His own strength. No human being can. Therefore, He would have to rely upon the power of the Holy Spirit; and He offered Himself through the Holy Spirit to God the Father, and God the Father then gave Jesus to make perfect His redemption plan.

Follow me very closely now. Watch the ministry of the three Persons. Watch Jesus and the complete and implicit faith that He had in the Holy Spirit. You know, sometimes I think—in fact, I am sure—that we talk too much about our own faith. The greatest example of faith in the Word of God that I know anything about is the faith that Jesus Himself illustrated in this connection with the other two members of the Trinity. Jesus had complete faith in the Father before that moment when He was conceived of the Holy Spirit in the womb of Mary. He also had complete faith in the keeping power of the Holy Spirit, and in the Holy Spirit's faithfulness to Him before He ever came to earth.

Now turn with me to a portion of the Word of God that tells us of the first time that all three persons of the Godhead are seen after Jesus offered Himself through the Holy Spirit to the Father to be given for our redemption. It's at the time of Jesus' water baptism, and it is found in

Matthew 3:16. "And Jesus, when he was baptized, went up straightway out of the water: and, lo, the heavens were opened unto him, and he saw the Spirit of God descending like a dove, and lighting upon him." (I believe this is the first time that Jesus had this personal connection with the Holy Spirit since that time when He was conceived of the Holy Spirit in the womb of Mary. We have no record of anything prior to this.)

Suddenly something happened. The heavens were opened and Jesus saw the Spirit of God descending like a dove and lighting upon Him. Don't you love it when the Holy Spirit is likened unto a dove, which is the gentlest and most sensitive of all birds? There is quietness and no confusion about a dove. The three Persons are again united. But something else happened: "And lo a voice from heaven [and the One who speaks is still in heaven—it is God the Father] saying, This is my beloved Son, in whom I am well pleased" (Matthew 3:17).

Here we have the three: first, we have God the Father speaking and saying, "This is My beloved Son." In other words God was confirming that this is the One who offered Himself through the Holy Spirit to the Father that He might be given for the redemption of lost men and women. At the same time, the Holy Spirit descended upon the Son of the living God. As Jesus, who was as much man as though He were not God, came up from out of the waters of baptism, the Holy Spirit was assuring Jesus that He was there to equip Him with power for service. He would be His Strengthener for the work He had to do as He represented the Father in person.

As Jesus walked this earth, He was literally and in reality God in the flesh walking this earth. The Holy Spirit came upon Jesus as Jesus was in the flesh, and He equipped Him with His wonderful power for service, literally filled that vessel with Himself and His power.

Is that all? Is that the end of it? No. We see the miracles of healing that Jesus did as He walked among men, and often we think of Jesus doing these things in *His* power. But it was not His own power. Look at Acts 10:38: "God anointed Jesus of Nazareth with the Holy Ghost and with power: who went about doing good, and healing all that were oppressed of the devil; for God was with him." Who did these great miracles? A man? No man can. No human being has the power. Jesus, as He walked this earth in the natural, as much man as though He were not God, could not have performed a miracle had it not been for the power of the Holy Spirit in Him and through Him. *God anointed Jesus of Nazareth with the Holy Ghost and with power.*

Beloved, that was the secret of the ministry of Jesus. Therein was the power for the miracles that Jesus performed. It was the power of the Holy Spirit working in and through Him. That is the reason Jesus spoke of the Holy Spirit. Jesus told those who were close to Him regarding the ministry of this wonderful One; and then, just before Jesus went away, He turned to them and His last words were the most important words that He could possibly speak to them. Why? He was going away, and He was leaving this great responsibility with them. What did He say just before His feet left the Mount of Olives? He turned to that little handful and said: "Ye shall receive power, after that the Holy Ghost is come upon you" (Acts 1:8).

Ye shall receive power—power to witness, power to do the very things that He had been doing, because this same wonderful Person, the Holy Spirit, will come. Jesus said that He would send Him unto us, and through Him we would have power to live a life of victory. It was never in Jesus' plan that anyone of His own, that any Christian, should live a life of defeat. Jesus lived an undefeated life when He walked this earth, and He said that this same secret of power that had been His would be ours now.

The Holy Spirit is given to the believer for one purpose and only one—to witness and for service. He was not given for personal spiritual picnics or enjoyment. Jesus never used the power and the person of the Holy Spirit for His own pleasure, and neither are we to use the person and power of the Holy Spirit for our own pleasure. The Holy Spirit was given to us to witness and for power for service, and we need to appropriate that which is ours today as members of His Body.

8

The Three Persons of the Trinity

I will always remember the response I received after preaching a message over the radio that God is a person in bodily form. Many folks wrote thanking me for having given the Scriptures and for proving from the Word of God that God is a person and is in bodily form. Many thought of Him as the very essence of all power, the great Ruler, one who had unlimited might, the great Creator. They thought Him to be something very mystical, but they did not consider Him a person in bodily form. Yet, the Word of God clearly teaches it and I am going to give you instances from the Bible where we have proof that God is in bodily form.

We read in the 33rd Chapter of Exodus that one day the Lord and Moses were having a heart-to-heart talk and the Lord told Moses that he was held in great favor. So Moses replied, in essence, "If I have truly found grace in Your sight, let me see You just once, let me look into Your face for an instant."

Now when Moses made this request, this is what God replied: "Thou canst not see my face: for there shall no man see me, and live" (Exodus 33:20).

Many a time I, too, have been human enough to have thought that if only for a minute I could see my Lord, I could go through anything. If for only a second I could look upon His face, everything would be fine.

Think of God's glory! Think of His power and righteousness! Our puny minds cannot fathom what the face of God must be like, or comprehend the full extent of His glory. No wonder in talking about the city of the New Jerusalem, the Book of the Revelation reads that there will be no need for the moon or the sun there because the glory of the Lord will light the entire place (Revelation 21:23).

The Lord continued to speak to Moses:

Thou canst not see my face: for there shall no man see me, and live.

And the Lord said, Behold, there is a place by me, and thou shalt stand upon a rock:

And it shall come to pass, while my glory passeth by, that I will put thee in a cleft of the rock, and will cover thee with my hand while I pass by:

> *And I will take away mine hand, and thou*
> *shalt see my back parts: but my face shall not be*
> *seen.*
>
> (Exodus 33:20-23)

Turn now to another portion of the Word in Genesis 1:26, when God said to the Son and the Holy Spirit: "Let us make man in our image, after our likeness." You and I, products of God's creation, are made in the image and likeness of God. Therefore, I believe with every atom of my being that God has a body, that God has hands, that God has a face. He is not something that is mystical or an unknown factor some place. If that was all I had on which to base my faith, I certainly would not be giving my life as a living sacrifice for what I believe.

We have seen that God is a very definite person in bodily form. We know that Jesus is a person, for when He left this earth, He did not go away as a spirit. His body ascended to heaven. He went away in bodily form—feet, hands, face—and He shall return in like manner as He was seen when He went away. That is what the angel of the Lord said, as recorded in Acts 1:11.

Now we come to the person of the Holy Spirit, one who also has a very definite personality, and this truth is something that is hard for some men and women to accept. The Holy Spirit is not just an attribute, not just a great influence, not a mystical force whose work is beyond our power to understand. How anyone can study the Word of God or read the Bible and not recognize the personality of the Holy Spirit, I will never know. The other day someone asked, "How is it that there is controversy regarding the Holy Spirit? " I have only one answer to give and it is simply this: it is due to a lack of teaching. One cannot come with an open heart and an open mind searching for the reality and truth regarding the Third Person of the Trinity without immediately recognizing this definite, this strong, this glorious invisible person of the Holy Spirit. He is vitally important to the life of every one of God's children.

There is a portion of God's Word, a real eye-opener regarding this Third Person of the Trinity, where Jesus is speaking. "I will pray the Father, and he shall give you another Comforter, that he may abide with you forever" (John 14:16). In essence Jesus is saying, "I'm going away. You have seen me here in person. I have been with you and I have taught you many things; but it is expedient for you that I go away because I have another position to fill, that of great High Priest. I cannot stay with you here on earth. I must leave. But do not be afraid for I will ask the Father to send you another Strengthener, an Advocate. I have tried to strengthen you and to teach you, but I will ask the Father to send you another who will not only teach you but will reveal me to you and commune with you. He will lead you and guide you. He is the Holy Spirit."

Throughout this 14th chapter of John, I want you to pay attention to the personal pronouns. You will see that every time Jesus referred to the Holy Spirit, every time He talked of the Holy Ghost, He always referred to Him as a person and a personal pronoun was used.

Then Jesus speaks these seven words, "that He may abide with you forever." I shall never forget the day when I saw those words and understood them as never before. Those words were spoken about the Holy Spirit. Therefore we must recognize the importance of the person who will abide with us, not for just a day nor a year, not for just the time of our life span here on earth, but *forever*. When we realize this fact, we'll understand as never before that this person of the Holy Spirit is one who is vitally important to each of us. You and I cannot ignore someone that Jesus said would be with us *forever*.

You see, since I have become acquainted with the Holy Spirit, He has come to mean so much in my life that I really don't know what I would do without Him. I mean that. We have been so closely associated, I do not know what I would do if, in God's great plan, He had said, "Now this Holy Spirit will only be with you for a limited span of time." I wouldn't want to spend eternity without Him. We have had such wonderful communion and fellowship here on earth. There have been those times of anointing and times when He has been my guide. He has given me the Father's wisdom. I am so glad the Father made provision that the Holy Spirit will never leave me.

But Jesus does not stop there. He continues by saying, "even the Spirit of truth: whom the world cannot receive, because it seeth him not, neither knoweth him." In other words, because the natural man has no eye for the Holy Spirit and no interest in Him, he cannot see or understand Him. Jesus continues, "but ye know him: for he dwelleth with you; and shall be in you" (John 14:17). First Jesus is talking to those in His presence, then He speaks about the future when He will go away and will take the position of great High Priest in heaven. Thus, the Holy Spirit is with every born-again Christian. If you have had that new birth experience, He is *with* you.

But, as I told you before, there is more : "He shall be *in* you," Jesus said. So whenever we speak of the Holy Spirit dwelling within us, that is scriptural. He is not only *with* me, but also *in* me. I could talk to you not only of His glorious presence with me , and I am conscious of His presence with me constantly, but Jesus promised that He would be *in* me .

The indwelling presence of the Holy Spirit is essential to a true knowledge of God and of Jesus Christ. It is important that you and I understand this because we are living in an hour, in a time, when so much emphasis is put on the Holy Spirit. It is a time when He is giving of Himself, and pouring out Himself in these last days in a greater measure than ever before. We are seeing the manifestation of His power around the world. Thousands and thousands of people who were never interested in this doctrine before are becoming interested in the Holy Spirit. There are countless men who are standing in their pulpits, recognizing the Holy Spirit for the first time, because they are seeing the results of His power. We cannot ignore the fact that we are seeing miracles today as we have never seen miracles before. We cannot close our eyes to the fact that there are literally hundreds and hundreds of people who are being filled with the Holy Ghost. We are living in the day when the things that happened in the early Church are again happening in our midst, the fruits and the gifts of the Spirit are being restored to the Church.

You may be asking the question, "Why?" It is because time is running out. The Holy Spirit is about to leave. We are coming to the end of this dispensation. Even as Jesus left, one of these days the Holy Spirit is going back to heaven again and He knows His time is short. He knows that very soon now the Church will be raptured, and He is literally working overtime. I do not mean to be sacrilegious when I say it, but that's exactly what is happening, and men and women are looking around and realizing something is taking place. They are aware that great changes are being made. And the answer to all the questions comes back: *It is the moving of the Holy Spirit.*

Everything I know about the Word of God and regarding spiritual things has come directly from the Bible, and it is the Holy Spirit who has been my teacher. When it comes to spiritual things, they are spiritually revealed, for Jesus Himself said, "He [the Holy Spirit] shall teach you all things, and bring all things to your remembrance whatsoever I have said unto you" (John 14:26).

In Luke 2:25 it is written, "And, behold, there was a man in Jerusalem, whose name was Simeon; and the same man was just and devout, waiting for the consolation of Israel, and the Holy Ghost was upon him."

It was the same Holy Spirit that we've been studying that came upon Simeon, for there is but *one* Holy Spirit. As we learned earlier, the Holy Spirit is not a new personality that came upon the scene at the Day of Pentecost. He is the same One who came upon the Old Testament saints and prophets and gave to them the revelations. Only *one* is the revealer of the deep truths of God—the Holy Spirit. He revealed these great truths to the Apostle Paul in the New Testament, and the same Holy Spirit is the revealer of the deep truths of God to you and to me today.

Back to Luke: "And it was revealed unto him [Simeon] by the Holy Ghost, that he should not see death, before he had seen the Lord's Christ. And he came by the Spirit [here is the Holy Spirit guiding him] into the temple: and when the parents brought in the child Jesus, to do for him after the custom of the law, then took he him up in his arms, and blessed God, and said, Lord, now lettest thou thy servant depart in peace, according to thy word: for mine eyes have seen thy salvation, which thou hast prepared before the face of all people; a light to lighten the Gentiles, and the glory of thy people Israel" (Luke 2:26-32).

Who gave the great revelation? Who guided Simeon? The Holy Spirit who still reveals truth to receptive hearts today, the One who will guide you and me on every side.

9

How to be Filled With the Holy Spirit

*I*n an earlier chapter, we saw that the indwelling Spirit was not universal, that the Old Testament saints had this experience when the Holy Spirit came upon them for special service and for special leadership—as in the lives of men like Moses, Gideon, and David. The gift came to them from God alone, and it was given only through His sovereignty. One of the great differences between the Old and the New Testaments is the changed relationship between the Spirit and God's people.

Jesus' disciples were in training with Him for three years, but not until the Day of Pentecost were they endued with power from on high. Peter, the fisherman, could never have preached the sermon he did on the Day of Pentecost and pierced 3000 in their hearts without the help of the Holy Spirit. The minister is to "rightly divide the word of truth" (2 Timothy 2:15), and Peter could not have done so if the Holy Spirit had not aided him.

The instrument that the Holy Spirit uses to convict and convert men and women is the Word of God. "The seed is the Word of God" (Luke 8:11). But, as in the natural world, the seed must be alive to germinate, and there can be no life without pre-existing life, for there is no such thing as spontaneous generation of life. So in the spiritual world the seed [the Word of God] must be vitalized by the Holy Spirit, otherwise it is barren.

A spiritual revelation cannot be comprehended by the natural understanding. Paul understood well when he said, "And my speech and my preaching was not with enticing words of man's wisdom, but in demonstration of the Spirit and of power" (1 Corinthians 2:4).

The new birth is the implantation of a new nature by the Spirit of God. It is the Holy Spirit who will take that one whose life has been regenerated and transformed by the power of God, and He will take the yielded and surrendered body and make it the temple of God in which He abides. He will use that body and use that life beyond the human mind's ability to comprehend.

The Baptism of the Holy Spirit is an occupancy. There is new strength, divine strength, and Holy Ghost boldness. There will be spiritual fruit that the Spirit gives; and I believe with all of my heart that everything that God gave the New Testament Church, all the fruits and gifts and graces of the

Holy Spirit, will be restored to the Church as the return of Christ draws near. Christ never intended to leave His Church powerless, for to this end "Christ . . . loved the church, and gave Himself for it . . . that he might present it to himself a glorious church" (Ephesians 5:25-27).

Now we come to the question that is asked of me again and again: *How can I be filled with the Spirit?* If you are a Christian and you have been born again, this second experience—the infilling of the Holy Spirit—is important to you and is a vital part of your spiritual growth, and a blessed part of your inheritance in Christ. It's God's plan that you receive this infilling of His Spirit.

In Ephesians 5:18, the Apostle Paul gives the command: "Be not drunk with wine, wherein is excess; but be filled with the Spirit." It's a command. It isn't optional. Read it for yourself: "be filled with the Spirit."

Now what does Paul have in mind when he said, "be filled with the Spirit"? This word "filled" may be used in two different senses. In the original text there are two different Greek words, both translated "filled." One suggests a filling up, as you might take a glass and a pitcher of water and you pour the water from the pitcher into the empty glass so that water fills up the glass. The disciples on the Day of Pentecost were filled—that is, they were filled with the Holy Spirit. The Spirit moved in, came in to dwell, and His presence was manifested in the believers. That is understandable.

But watch something. The second sense of the word seems to have the added thought not only of presence but of power that manifests itself through the individual who is filled up. It is not only that water was poured into the empty glass, but there was more than that. There was a power that manifested itself through that glass having been filled up with water. Thus, there is a place where one is so filled up with not only the *presence* of the Holy Spirit, but also filled up with a *power* that manifests itself, so that through

51

that individual who is filled up with the Spirit, Christ is revealed.

The power and presence of the Holy Spirit produces a new life. We see, therefore, that one can yield himself completely to the power and the person of the Holy Spirit to the extent where the Holy Spirit will control his life and being.

The question is often asked, "How can you know whether or not one has been filled with the Holy Spirit?" The Spirit produces a new walk, a new speech, and a new manner of life. There will be power in that life. That life will be dominated and controlled by the Holy Spirit.

That may generate another question of yours: *"How can I be filled with the Spirit?"* I will give the answer to you in just a few words: *Turn yourself and all you have over to Jesus.* You may ask, "Is it that simple?" *It is that simple!*

To turn over yourself and all you have to Jesus is the crucial point, and if you bungle this you will block the whole thing. You cannot love fully, work fully, where there is an unsurrendered self.

So, between you and Jesus there can be no love without an inward self-surrender. You cannot be filled with the Holy Spirit until there is an inward surrender of all that you are and all that you have. That means the real *you* surrendered to Him, not just the surrender of this thing or that thing. Some people miss it entirely by saying, "I surrendered this thing—or I surrendered another thing." It is not the surrender of *things*. It is the surrender of *you*!

The Holy Spirit fills that which you surrender unto Him. All that He wants is *you*. You do not seek Him. You do not seek something. You do not seek an evidence. You turn *yourself* over to Him, you commit yourself, you surrender yourself. It is an inward self-surrender to Jesus, and when you have surrendered to Him completely, the Holy Spirit will fill your vessel. He will not only fill it to the full, but there will be the outward manifestation of the power of that One who has filled you with Himself.

Being filled with the Spirit is that simple. There is no power in the world today greater than the power of the Holy Spirit, and when the blood of Christ and the power of the Holy Ghost are linked together, we have an energy that nothing can stop. *We have a power that produces miracles!*

I pray that *you* will know this blessed joy in your own life!

10

The Evidence of Being Filled With the Holy Spirit

he question has been asked, "At the time a believer is filled with the Holy Spirit, will there always be a visible and an outward manifestation of God's power upon that one?" The answer to that is, "Yes." But there is a companion to that question: "Can there be times when the Holy Spirit is received by faith, without any outward evidence?" The answer to that is, "No."

Now hold steady a moment before you disagree with me. I have given you a direct "Yes" and a direct "No" to these questions; but perhaps my answers mean something different than you may think. So, let us examine something that is most marvelous and important to every believer.

Begin with the question to which I answered, "No." When it comes to the new birth experience, one receives that experience by faith, for the Bible states that "by grace are ye saved through faith" (Ephesians 2:8). You accept by faith that which Jesus did on the Cross for you—the shedding of His blood and the giving of His life. He is the very Son of the Living God, and He made atonement for your soul and my soul, and by faith we accept that which Jesus did on the Cross. We are saved by fact, not by feeling.

Let me put it this way. A governor may issue a pardon to someone, and on that pardon there is affixed the Seal of the State. As a result, when that person who is condemned to die reaches out and accepts that pardon, he is a free man. He was not freed by any emotion. But when the fact of his freedom dawns upon that man who had no hope or future and was condemned to die, he will show emotion. That person will have feeling—he will experience unspeakable joy. But he was not freed because of his feelings or his emotions. He was freed when he was offered a pardon and he accepted that pardon.

In the same way, when a man or woman comes to the Lord Jesus Christ, that one is not saved by some emotional experience. I have known people to come to an altar every time an altar call was given. No matter who was the evangelist or preacher, that person made his way down the aisle. You could ask, "Didn't you accept Christ as your Savior last week?" And I have heard the answer, "I came but nothing happened. I felt nothing." And that person will go through life waiting for some emotional experience.

Remember something: that emotional experience or that feeling comes after you realize what actually happened when, by faith, you accepted that which Jesus did for you on the Cross. You and I are saved on facts, not on emotion, and those who live by their emotions waver and vacillate when the winds of controversy blow and the storms of life come. Because they live by their emotions, you will find them up one day and down the next day. One day they think they're saved, and the next day they're not sure if they are. You find them steeped in unbelief, and every time there's a new doctrine preached they go for it hook, line, and sinker. In the final analysis, they don't know what they believe.

But give me a man or a woman who has accepted Jesus Christ on bare facts, and it is literally the greatest transaction that a human being can know. That person is saved on facts, facts that he accepts by faith. And when that person knows what and why he believes and can point to the Word of God and say, "It is right here in the Bible," you will never find that one wavering. He is solid and knows that his salvation is real.

Now let us consider another result of the born-again experience. There will also be an outward evidence regarding that person's salvation. How do we know that person has truly been born again, that he is a new creature in Christ Jesus? By the fact that his thinking and way of living are changed. He has a new sense of values, and a different outlook on life and everything that pertains to life. "Old things are passed away; behold, all things are become new" (2 Corinthians 5-17).

The amazing thing is this—the individual himself may not realize this terrific change that has happened to him because of his experience, but his family will see it. The neighbors will see it. The man who used to curse and swear may not realize that he is going around whistling instead.

Nobody ever heard him whistle before or ever saw him so happy. He doesn't realize that he is anxious to get to church when he never darkened a church door before.

Here is a true incident that is typical of such a person. One of our ushers came to me and said, "You know, one of our new ushers shook hands with me six times this morning and has 'God blessed' me each time. I have known that man for years and never before has he 'God blessed' anyone prior to his wonderful experience of salvation." You see, the things that man once hated, he now loves. He loves the Word of God and there is an outward evidence of that which has taken place on the inside of him. That is the new birth.

Now we come to this experience of being filled with the Holy Spirit. One may ask. "Why can't a person be filled with the Holy Spirit when they're born again?" I will be perfectly honest with you and tell you something: *I don't think any of us could stand it!* Do you want to know why I say that? In the first place, our old physical bodies are not geared for such power and for such a radical change. Think it over yourself.

If you're acquainted with my radio broadcasts, perhaps you heard the testimony of the Jewish Rabbi who had been listening to my messages on the Holy Spirit. It was all so wonderful and new to him, and so he stood on the platform of the Shrine Auditorium in Los Angeles one Sunday and publicly took his stand, accepting Jesus as the true Messiah. A week or so later, he wrote me and he said, "Please continue to pray for my friend, John, but please discontinue your prayers for me."

That was all he said and I was terribly disturbed. When I returned to the Shrine Auditorium the next month, here was my precious Rabbi friend. He came to me prior to the start of the service and said, "I want to explain something. I'm sure you received my letter asking you to pray for John, but not for me. You see. I asked you to withhold your prayers for me just a little while until I could get better acclimated to this new life. This wonderful spiritual thing that has happened to me is so overwhelming. It has come with such great force upon me that I cannot absorb any more just yet. So don't pray any more for me until I get used to this new life and a little more accustomed to it. Then you can start praying for me again that I might receive more."

One cannot take all that God has for him at once. The experience of being filled with the Holy Spirit is as definite as the new birth experience, and this infilling of the Spirit has nothing to do with a person's salvation. Please note that the filling of the Holy Spirit is given for an entirely different purpose than the salvation of the soul. When a person is born again, that person accepts the work that Jesus did for him on the Cross by faith. When death comes, the soul goes all the way from earth to glory, leaving this old body of clay, and the spirit is present with the Lord.

This second experience, being filled with the Holy Spirit, has nothing to do with salvation. It is for the purpose of service. As Christians, we are saved to serve. Those of us who are born of the Spirit, heirs of God, born into the body of Christ, must be equipped with power for service.

Perhaps you have heard me say this before, for I often liken our hearts to a compartment having many separate rooms. At the time of our conversion, we accept that pardon and we open the door of one of the rooms of our heart. We say, "Come in, dear Jesus," and then the blood of Jesus Christ, God's Son, cleanses us from all sin. Conversion is instantaneous, but the Christ-life is a spiritual growth. You do not receive everything there is as a result of one experience.

But after you have opened the first door to Jesus, you soon find that you are opening the door of another room of your heart, then another. As you continue to consecrate and walk in the light as Jesus is in the light, there comes a time in this spiritual growth that you look up and literally and honestly say, "None of self, but all of Thee, Lord." Finally, after you have surrendered everything to Him, it is then that the Holy Spirit comes in and you experience the Baptism of the Holy Spirit.

Jesus spoke to Nicodemus and compared the new birth to the way that a baby is born. Nicodemus questioned it and asked, "How can a man enter a second time into his mother's womb, and be born?" (John 3:4). A baby, this little tiny bit of flesh, can be born a perfect physical specimen with nothing wrong with that bundle of flesh. But, if that baby is not fed or is not given the right food, it can become emaciated and its growth is stunted.

In exactly the same way there is spiritual growth. There must be the feeding of the inward spiritual person, and there is no better spiritual food for the spiritual person than the Word of God. It literally is the spiritual person's food for growth. There must be a constant and continual growth of the spiritual person, but there can be no growth until first the man himself has been born again. And when there is the surrender to Christ of body, soul, and spirit, then that person receives this glorious infilling of the Holy Spirit.

Always remember, there is no vacuum in nature. Let me make an analogy here. Imagine a beautiful vase of flowers with water in the vase. If you turn the vase upside down, the flowers and the water in the vase will fall to the ground. After the last drop of water leaves the container, you may say, "Look, the vase is empty." But not really. The second that the flowers and the water left the container, air rushed in and filled the vase because there is no vacuum in nature.

In exactly the same way, when the human heart or life begins to be emptied of self and we surrender to God our minds and bodies as a living sacrifice, it is then that we are filled with the Holy Spirit. It is the presenting of our body as a vessel for the Holy Spirit to use for the glory of God. It is then, when we surrender our selfish motives and desires, and surrender our will to Him, that we have no will of our own. We live to please Him. Our body becomes the temple of the Holy Spirit, a vessel that is filled with the Holy Ghost, and He comes in and uses our mind, our tongue, our hands, our body. Our will becomes not a will that is separate and apart from the will of God. We are so surrendered that we have one will, and that will is the will of the Father. The Holy Spirit now directs the Father's will through our lives.

Being filled with the Holy Spirit, the experience that we call the Baptism of the Holy Spirit, is a work that the Holy Spirit does in us, so that through us He might be a Power for service. We cannot receive this all-important experience and not know it. We do not receive the Baptism of the Holy Spirit, the infilling experience of the Holy Ghost, by faith—*we receive it by surrender.*

All right, what did Jesus say just before He went away? He promised, "Ye shall receive power, after that the Holy Ghost is come upon you" (Acts 1:8), and you do not receive this power by faith. You do not receive this glorious dynamite, this magnificent dynamo, by faith. You do not come in contact with this glorious power by faith.

Let me explain. Look at the second chapter of the Book of Acts. As they tarried there in that Upper Room, they received nothing by faith. By faith they went into the Upper Room. By faith they accepted that which Jesus had promised. But their tarrying was mighty real, and when they came out of that Upper Room, not one of them had accepted that experience by faith. *Something really happened!* Was there an outward evidence of it? I told you before that when one is born again, there very definitely is an outward evidence. That person is a new creature in Jesus Christ and everybody will know it if you have truly been born again. In exactly the same way, there will be an outward evidence of the filling with the Holy Ghost if you have had that experience.

Let me use a certain person as an example. You may guess that I am speaking of Peter when I say that one day there was a man so cowardly, so weak, that a little damsel frightened him into denying that he knew Jesus. In the second chapter of Acts, however, we see the evidence of Peter having been filled with the Holy Ghost, for he went out of that Upper Room with Holy Ghost boldness and began preaching and said, "Repent, and be baptized everyone of you in the name of Jesus Christ for the remission of sins, and ye shall receive the gift of the Holy Ghost" (Acts 2:38).

Was there evidence of Peter having been filled with the Holy Spirit? *We can't deny it!* Look at the Holy Ghost boldness that Peter displayed. In Acts 2:41 we read, "Then they that gladly received his word were baptized: and the same day there were added unto them about three thousand souls."

Peter did not accept the promise of the Holy Spirit by faith. He accepted the Word of Jesus by faith. He tarried, and there were visible manifestations of the power of God. Then, when he walked out of that Upper Room, he knew he had been filled, and there was scriptural and biblical evidence of his experience. There was Holy Ghost boldness as the Holy Ghost spoke through him—it was the Holy Ghost in him using him.

Please let me share an experience I had, which I believe will make my point clear. I begin by giving you a Scripture, the words of Jesus, that have meant much to me: "He that loseth his life for my sake shall find it" (Matthew 10:39). I have preached many sermons on the first part—"he that loseth his life for my sake," but I have never put emphasis on the last part: "shall find it."

I remember well the end of McChesney Road in Portland, Oregon. At that time it was a dead-end street. It was four o'clock one Saturday afternoon when I literally felt I had lost my life to Christ because that was the hour years ago when I literally, and for all time, surrendered my will to God's will.

Then one day in the Civic Auditorium in Portland, the same city where I lost my will to God's will, I stood on the stage and saw a man stand to his feet, a man who had been in a wheelchair with multiple sclerosis for nine years. I witnessed the healing power of the Lord Jesus Christ flow through his body, making him completely whole. It was a time of great rejoicing as we witnessed God's power in action. Those who saw that great miracle, however, never dreamed what the Holy Spirit was saying to me. He said, "You lost your life for My sake, but you found it in Him." *Beloved, I found my life, for I lost my will to His will.*

This same glorious power is available to you today. The Holy Spirit will use all who will surrender to Jesus— all who will invite Him to fill them with His power to witness and to serve. Hallelujah!

11

The Holy Spirit Within Us

*O*nce again, let me remind you that there is no greater power in the world than the power of the Holy Spirit.

We have seen that before Jesus returned to heaven, He left to His Church the greatest gift that He could possibly have left—the Holy Spirit. In giving the Church this gift,

He promised, "And ye shall receive power" (Acts 1:8). In other words, Jesus was saying, "I give you the same power that was manifested in My life on earth, the same power that was manifested in My ministry. You have seen the miracles. You have seen the demonstration of supernatural power. Now I am going away, but I am not leaving you powerless. As a gift, I am giving to you, My own Church, the same power that was mine when I walked this earth."

In view of this promise made by our Lord, let me ask you: *What are you doing with this power?* What are you doing with this wonderful gift? What are you doing in the world today with the Holy Spirit—with the greatest gift that was possible for Jesus to give? Thousands of God's professing children are living defeated, powerless lives. In some instances, they're almost bringing a reproach on the gospel of the Lord Jesus Christ because they're living lives of defeat. I ask you again: *What are you doing with this gift?*

Look in your Bible at 2 Corinthians 13:11-14. Before we consider this portion of Scripture, however, let me remind you that these words were written during a very trying era in the life of the great Apostle Paul. It was a time of physical weakness, weariness, suffering, and pain. Sometimes we tend to forget that this spiritual giant had not yet put on immortality. His body of flesh was not immune to sickness or suffering, and neither was it immune to temptation. That's one of the reasons it's very cruel to point a finger and say that sickness or suffering or trials are always a result of sin in the life of one of God's children. Paul was one of the greatest saints who ever lived and, as a result, God entrusted to him spiritual revelations beyond what was ever given to any other human being. God had confidence in him.

In 2 Corinthians 13:11-14, Paul wrote:

> *Finally, brethren, farewell. Be perfect, be of*
> *good comfort, be of one mind, live in peace; and the*
> *God of love and peace shall be with you. . . .*
>
> *The grace of the Lord Jesus Christ, and the love*
> *of God, and the communion of the Holy Ghost, be*
> *with you all. Amen.*

Here Paul begins by exhorting all Christians to grow into maturity in God, to be perfect in spite of pain and afflictions, and in spite of their suffering and temptations. We are still in the world but not of this world, living in an old body of flesh. *Yet, we are challenged to be perfect.* How can that be? We agree that such a thing as perfection in one's self is impossible, but Paul was talking about the perfection of Jesus Christ the Son of the Living God. We can consecrate and we can give Him all there is of us. But remember something, our perfection is in the perfection of Jesus Christ as we continue to stand perfect in the love of God. So, be of good comfort in spite of your suffering and temptations. He is with you and in you to bring you victory.

Paul goes on, "Be of one mind and live in peace." In other words, he is saying that no matter what happens to you, you are God's child. You belong to Him. There is a place in the center of His will where you can continue to be perfect. So we can be of good comfort and of one mind, having the mind of Christ and not a divided mind. God's Word charges us to be steadfast, to know what we believe and stick with it, and the only place in the world where one finds real peace of mind is where there is the peace of God. We need to come back again to the real and true values of spiritual things.

Now we come to Paul's closing words: "the grace of the Lord Jesus Christ, and the love of God, and the communion of the Holy Ghost, be with you all. Amen."

Every Sunday morning this portion of Scripture is repeated in literally thousands of holy sanctuaries, and yet few understand the full meaning of those words. The greatest saint living this hour cannot fully comprehend the real depth of their meaning, for who can fathom the grace of the Lord Jesus Christ? His grace is greater than all our sins—is greater than all of our failures.

The longer I live, the more I am aware of His grace. His grace amazes me.

Take for example a man or woman who has never served God a day in their life. I have seen such people instantly and gloriously healed by the power of God. But not only is the body touched, their sins are forgiven and the joy of the Lord floods them body and soul. It was not because of any merit or any goodness on the part of that person, but the grace and mercy of the Lord Jesus Christ.

Neither can we fathom the love of God. No human tongue or pen can tell or describe the depth of the love of God. He loves us with an everlasting love, a love that forgives, a love that protects, a love that surrounds, a love that provides, a love that defends, a love that adopts, a love that has made you and me His heirs and joint-heirs with His only begotten Son. If only we could catch a vision of the love of God, and you and I as Christians and God's children could somehow show the world an example of His love because we're a part of Him and a part of His nature, countless others would be led to Christ. We represent Him before the world: "For to me to live is Christ" (Philippians 1:21). You and I are often the only Jesus the sinner sees. Therefore, for us to live is Christ, and through our lives we must show His love in the things that we do.

But Paul does not stop there. He goes on, "And the communion of the Holy Ghost, be with you all." Next Lord's Day, if everyone who repeats this portion of the Word of God would understand the full meaning of these Words as they stand in God's divine presence, we would have a new America. That is all that men and women would need, the full meaning and consciousness of all that is involved in this one verse: *the communion of the Holy Ghost.* Do you understand what it means that you and I, frail creatures of the dust, may have fellowship and commune with the Holy Ghost?

That is why I told you earlier that only those who have received the Baptism of the Holy Spirit and have been filled with the Holy Spirit have a true knowledge of the Holy Spirit. It is a communion that is constant. In that midnight hour when it is so dark and you lie there awake and you are conscious of a presence that is so close to you that He is a vital part of even your breathing, there is no fear. There is no worry. You find yourself in close fellowship with a person, the Holy Spirit, a presence that is closer to you than even the beating of the heart within your body.

Have you stood before the open grave of a loved one that has been taken and found that you feel no frustration, only peace and hope? Your tears may water the flowers that lie on the casket; but there is a joy, His joy, way down deep. You are conscious of a Strengthener, the Comforter, even as you leave the graveside and go home to an empty house. Sure there is loneliness. You are human. But there is no fear. There is hope. There is peace. Beloved, you understand, it is the communion with the Comforter, your Strengthener, the Holy Spirit.

The Holy Spirit is not only the mighty Comforter. He also lifts up a standard against your enemy, and not one of God's children need be defeated on a single score. The Word of God promises: "So shall they fear the name of the Lord from the west, and his glory from the rising of the sun. When the enemy shall come in like a flood, the Spirit of the Lord shall lift up a standard against him" (Isaiah 59:19).

Our Lord and Savior has made provision for victory for everyone of His own. Not one of us needs ever go down in defeat, not for a second, for when the enemy shall come in like a flood, the Spirit of the Lord, the Holy Spirit, the Holy Ghost, shall lift up a standard against him. You do not fight your own battles. I do not fight my own battles. *The Spirit of the Lord, the Holy Ghost, fights our battles for us!*

12

Unlimited Power

*J*esus knew the importance and the unlimited power of the Holy Spirit. He understood this glorious person and He knew His personality well. That was the reason He could trust Him and before He ever came to earth to take upon Himself the form of man, He committed Himself to be given through the Holy Spirit. That is why over and over again during the ministry of Jesus, the Scriptures tell us that the Holy

Ghost was upon Him, and those great miracles that Jesus performed were a result of the power of the Holy Spirit.

This explains why I believe you and I should not discredit the manifestation of the supernatural power of the Holy Spirit today. Why is it when I tell someone to believe God for a miracle in his own life that it is often hard for that person to accept? The power of the Holy Spirit is the greatest force in the world. It always amazes me how much Peter and Paul and the Old Testament saints knew regarding this Third Person of the Trinity. They were absolutely dependent upon the Holy Spirit, and you and I should have that same nearness, the same consciousness of His power as they had. We have every right to know just as much about the power of the Holy Spirit as those Christians in the early church, for Peter said, "We have not followed cunningly devised fables [I like the way that is expressed], when we made known unto you the power and coming of our Lord Jesus Christ, but were eyewitnesses of his majesty" (2 Peter 1:16).

Pause a minute. What was Peter talking about and referring to when he wrote, "But we were eyewitnesses of his majesty"? He was talking about that wonderful experience they had on the Mount of Transfiguration when Jesus took Peter, James, and John, and brought them up into a high mountain apart, and was transfigured before them (Matthew 17:1-2). Peter was saying that he was an eyewitness, that it was not a hallucination that he had. Peter was willing to stake his very life on it, I'm sure. All the forces of hell could not have argued Peter out of what he saw.

It is true today—I have seen it. One can witness the manifestation of God's power, that great invisible force, and when he tells someone else about the miracle, someone who was not present, that one will often use every means to explain it away as an emotional experience or hypnotism or offer some other reason to account for what really took place by the power of the Holy Spirit.

Had you approached Peter and said to him that it couldn't be that he saw Moses and Elijah, that it was absolutely impossible, Peter would have replied, "I was an eyewitness!" An eyewitness to what? In answer to that, Matthew 17:2-4: "And Jesus was transfigured before them: and his face did shine as the sun, and his raiment was white as the light, and, behold, there appeared unto them Moses and Elijah talking with him [the Master]. Then answered Peter, and said unto Jesus, Lord, it is good for us to be here: if thou wilt, let us make here three tabernacles; one for thee, and one for Moses, and one for Elijah."

Peter was so excited with what he saw that he got so carried away he couldn't keep quiet. I can almost hear him say, "This is the greatest thing that ever happened to me! It's an experience I don't want to forget. Let us do something about the whole thing. Let us make three tabernacles: one for Jesus, one for Moses, and one for Elijah. Let's start building now!"

The Scripture passage goes on, "While he yet spake, behold, a bright cloud overshadowed them: and behold a voice out of the cloud, which said, This is my beloved Son, in whom I am well pleased; hear ye him" (Matthew 17:5). No one told Peter to be quiet, but God caught his attention by a cloud and a voice out of the cloud. That will get your attention every time.

And Peter kept quiet. "And when the disciples heard it, they fell on their face, and were sore afraid" (Matthew 17:6). Peter fell on his face and I believe with every atom of my being that it was the power of the Holy Spirit that caused Peter and James and John to fall on their faces. Yes, they were sore afraid.

But isn't it just like Jesus to comfort them: "And Jesus came and touched them, and said, Arise, and be not afraid. And when they had lifted up their eyes, they saw no man, save Jesus only. And as they came down from the mountain, Jesus charged them, saying, Tell the vision to no man, until the Son of man be risen again from the dead." (Matthew 17:7-9).

This experience is what Peter was referring to when he said, "We were eyewitnesses of his majesty (2 Peter 1:16). He had seen with his very own eyes: "for he received from God the Father honor and glory, when there came such a voice to him, from the excellent glory." Then Peter repeats exactly the words of the Father that they heard with their ears on the Mount of Transfiguration, and he quotes God the Father's Words, "This is my beloved Son, in whom I am well pleased. And this voice which came from heaven we heard, when we were with him in the holy mount" (2 Peter 1:17-18). Peter could not be argued out of what he saw, nor the voice he heard when he and James and John were with Jesus on the holy mountain.

Yes, both the Old Testament prophets and those in the New Testament wrote and taught as they were moved by the Holy Ghost, and today the same Holy Spirit is still moving upon men and women, revealing Jesus to hungry and thirsty hearts.

13

The Holy Spirit Intercedes

*I*t always amazes me that there are thousands of Christians who do not see the importance of the Holy Spirit. Do you realize just how important the Holy Spirit really is? The Bible tells us that there is a sin for which there is no forgiveness. It's a sin not against God the Father nor against Jesus Christ the Son, but against the person of the Holy Spirit. That fact makes Him a very important person. A sin committed against God the Father can be forgiven. Any sin committed against Jesus Christ the Son will be forgiven. But the sin against the Holy Spirit will not be forgiven in this world or in the world to come. *That's how important and sacred He is.*

> *Wherefore I say unto you, All manner of sin and blasphemy shall be forgiven unto men: but the blasphemy against the Holy Ghost shall not be forgiven unto men.*
>
> *And whosoever speaketh a word against the Son of man, it shall be forgiven him: but whosoever speaketh against the Holy Ghost, it shall not be forgiven him, neither in this world, neither in the world to come.*
> (Matthew 12:31-32)

Remember something. Very often the hardest thing in the world is to know the perfect will of God. You have experienced it, and I have too. If you have been born again, if you love the Lord with all of your heart and you know the things of the Spirit, then more than anything in the world you desire God's perfect will. Yet, sometimes it is the hardest thing in the world to know the perfect will of God.

To begin with let me remind you that as long as you are in God's perfect will, you will know peace, even when the waters are deep and the storms rage. I'll admit that when you walk by the will of God, there will not always be sunshine. The will of God may not always bring you material prosperity or lead in the paths where it is easy. Sometimes God's guiding hand will direct you through deep waters, and sometimes you may feel those waters are about to overflow. The will of God may steer you through dark nights, where you cannot see His face and where you can scarcely hear His voice. You may feel alone like John on the Isle of Patmos. Have you wondered as I have if John ever questioned if that was God's perfect will for him? Or whether Paul ever pondered if those prison walls were God's perfect will for him? One thing I can assure you of and it is this: when you are in God's perfect will, there will be peace. You will have power and later the glory.

Aside from God's perfect will, however, there is such a thing as God's permissive will. In this regard let us read a couple of verses of the Scriptures where David speaks of the children of Israel.

> *He rebuked the Red Sea also, and it was dried up: so he led them through the depths, as through the wilderness.*
>
> *And he saved them from the hand of him that hated them, and redeemed them from the hand of the enemy.*
>
> *And the waters covered their enemies: there was not one of them left.*
>
> *Then believed they his words; they sang his praise.*
>
> *They soon forgat his works; they waited not for his counsel:*
>
> *But lusted exceedingly in the wilderness, and tempted God in the desert.*
>
> *And he gave them their request; but sent leanness into their soul*

(Psalm 106:9-15)

God gave the children of Israel their request, but in granting their request that was not His perfect will for them, it brought leanness to their souls. Their request was only God's second best for them, His permissive but not His perfect will, for they refused to pay the price for His perfect will. There are many who will read these words who have lived most of their lifetime according to God's permissive will, His second best. Perhaps there was less of a sacrifice to be made, so they chose the easy way.

See something. I know you may have struggled with this thing regarding the will of God, and this could be vitally important to you. I have been in the same predicament many times in my life, and I can only give to you what I have experienced myself.

What do I do? First of all, at the very beginning I seek to get my heart into such a state that it has no will of its own about a given matter. I'm just as human as you are, and I tell you frankly that is one of the hardest things in the world. When we face something and we are desperate about making the right decision, it is not easy to get our own personal feelings out of the situation. Invariably there is one thing we would rather do than another. We have our likes. We have our dislikes. But we can never know God's perfect will until we get our hearts and our minds in such a state that we have no will of our own in regard to a given matter.

I have learned that nine-tenths of our troubles are just here—nine-tenths of our difficulties are overcome when our hearts are ready to do God's will whatever it may be. When one is truly in this state, it is usually but a little way to the knowledge of what His will is. If right now you are struggling with the will of God, I urge you to get your mind and heart to the position where you have no will of your own. Then it will take only a short while before you will know God's perfect will.

Having done this, do not leave the result to feeling or simple impression. To do so would make you liable to delusions. Some people govern their life by feelings and that is why they get themselves into such desperate situations. There are times when we all have brought our troubles on ourselves because we allow our emotions and our feelings to govern us. Don't do it. If your decisions are based on feelings or simple impressions or emotions, you will make yourself liable to great delusions.

What is next? Seek the will of the Spirit of God through the Word of God, *for His will for you will never be contrary to His Word.* That is one thing you can be dead sure of. He will never make you an exception to His Word. His Word stands true. His will always will be in accordance with His✝ Word.

Now you may have come to the place where, after having done all these things, you still do not know God's perfect will. Here is where the Holy Spirit comes in. He intercedes. "Likewise the Spirit also helpeth our infirmities: for we know not what we should pray for as we ought: but the Spirit itself maketh intercession for us with groanings which cannot be uttered" (Romans 8:26).

Stop and say, "I do not know how to pray," and in that moment as you surrender yourself to the Spirit, He will present you and your need before the Father's throne. The Holy Spirit knows the perfect mind and the perfect will of God. He who searches your heart and knows you better than you know yourself will bring that need before the throne of God, and you cannot miss when the Holy Spirit prays through you. Please learn that secret, I beg you. Therefore, until you know God's perfect will, do absolutely nothing. Make no decision whatsoever. Be quiet and let the Holy Spirit intercede for you before the throne of God, and He will not fail you.

✱ in Eucharist

14

The Spirit-Filled Life

*M*y son, forget not my law; but let thine heart keep my commandments:

For length of days, and long life, and peace, shall they add to thee.

Let not mercy and truth forsake thee: bind them about thy neck; write them upon the table of thine heart:

> *So shalt thou find favour and good understanding in the sight of God and man.*
>
> *Trust in the LORD with all thine heart; and lean not unto thine own understanding.*
>
> *In all thy ways acknowledge him, and he shall direct thy paths.*
>
> (Proverbs 3:1-6)

What is the magic formula for a successful life? Have you ever asked yourself that question? Have you ever stopped to wonder why some people know success and others live and die a failure? What is this magic formula?

If you will turn to the Scriptures, you will find the answer outlined and described again and again, not just in the above portion of the Word of God, but over and again the formula for successful living is found in the Word of God. The writers of the Scriptures are the greatest writers who ever held a pen, and I have found that in only a few verses they can paint a story that would take a modern fiction writer hundreds of pages to relate. What did these men of God possess? It was the deep essence of the great truths in understanding people. They were inspired by the Holy Ghost, who knows mankind better than man knows himself.

There is a portion of the Scriptures that I have read many times regarding Peter and John. When we consider these two we must admit that they are a strange pair. There was John who was even tempered, and there was Peter who was always getting mad. At the drop of a hat he would get irritated, and I believe that if somebody didn't drop a hat, he became annoyed just the same. He never seemed to have control over himself.

Into these two lives a great change had come, and one day as recorded in Acts 3:1, they were going to the temple to pray. On the steps of the temple they encountered a beggar sitting with his hands outstretched begging for alms. Lame from birth with withered limbs, he was carried there every morning and carried back to his home at night. He would sit there all day long, waiting and crying, "Alms! Alms!" Yes, people dropped coins in his hands, but that did not solve his problem. Had every person who passed by him given him everything they possessed, it still would not have solved his problem, for it was not solely one of money but one of defeat. Peter and John could have turned their pockets inside out though their pockets may not have held very much, but even that would not have provided what this man needed. He still would have been lame.

In watching the beggar, they noticed that he failed to look up at the passing people. He had been at that place by the temple day after day, month after month, year after year. He was a common sight to everybody who passed by. No doubt John and Peter glanced at each other and thought to themselves, "We could be like this poor fellow." So Peter, always the first to speak up, said to the beggar, "Look on us!" (Acts 1:4). In Peter's voice I believe that there was an unmistakable something—a power, but something more than power. There was love, and love is something that comes through if it is the love of God in the person being used.

That love that came through in Peter's voice caused the beggar to slowly and painfully lift up his head until his weak, watery eyes met Peter's level gaze. Peter's face was kindly, lined but strong, a face weather-beaten by days on the sea of Galilee. But there was also a light upon it, a light from within. Peter and John had been filled with the Holy Spirit when He fell upon them in that Upper Room. They were among those who had been with one accord when the Spirit came upon them. They had heard that mighty sound of the rushing wind. They were there, and now the Holy Spirit was not only with them, He was in them. Out of their innermost being was flowing a river of living water, and as the beggar looked on them, he knew there was something different about them—there was a power in their words.

Can *you* say "look at me" to a defeated person? Are you so filled with the Holy Ghost and with the power of God that even without a word something radiates from that life of yours? As a mother, are you so living a Spirit-filled life that you do not have to preach and nag your unsaved husband or your unsaved daughter or that teen-age son? There is a magnetism that draws that unsaved and defeated person to Jesus Christ.

Then Peter spoke to the beggar, "In the Name of Jesus Christ of Nazareth, rise up and walk" (Acts 3:6). The man could hardly believe what he was hearing. He might have thought, *but I've been lame from youth—it is impossible!*

You know, sometimes people who have been long imprisoned, though they think they hate their chains and pray for freedom, really do not have the courage to be free. Peter repeated his command, "In the Name of Jesus of Nazareth rise up and walk." Then the man reached out his hand to Peter, who took it in his hand. The beggar rested his full weight upon ankle bones that had never been used before and the look of amazement, of joy, of gladness in his eyes cannot be described. "And He leaping up stood, and walked, and entered with them into the temple, walking, and leaping, and praising God" (Acts 3:8).

All through history this power has been lifting people. Undoubtedly there are those reading these words this very moment who have lived so long in skepticism they do not believe that this thing ever happened. They do not believe that there is a miraculous power in the universe, the greatest force in the world, the supernatural power of the Holy Spirit. Oh, my friend, it is real. *It is real!*

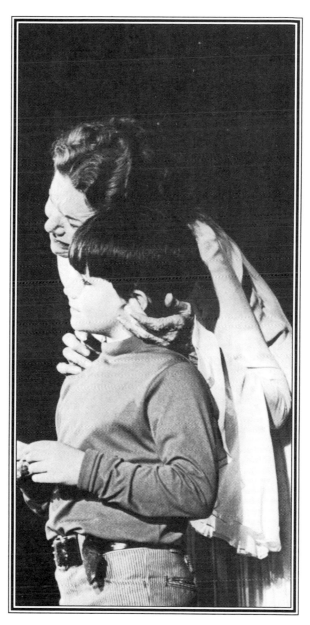

Miracle Service at Kiel Auditorium, St. Louis, April, 1975.

Mrs. Joe Kuhlman holding Geneva, Myrtle (behind mother), and Kathryn.

Baptismal Service at Brady's Run Park, 1958.

Private audience with Pope Paul, October 11, 1972.

Kathryn Kuhlman in Jerusalem, 1974.

Kathryn with students of a roof-top school in Hong Kong.

Kathryn Kuhlman at a Miracle Service.

Kathryn ministers during another Miracle Service,late 1970's.

Modern science has introduced many innovations to our everyday world, powers we never dreamed possible even twenty-five or thirty years ago. But there is a power that is greater than any earthly power. It is the power of the Holy Spirit, and it was demonstrated as Peter and John reached out to the beggar.

> *My son, forget not my law; but let thine heart keep my commandments:*
>
> *For length of days, and long life, and peace, shall they add to thee.*
>
> *Let not mercy and truth forsake thee: bind them about thy neck; write them upon the table of thine heart:*
>
> *So shalt thou find favor and good understanding in the sight of God and man.*
>
> *Trust in the Lord with all thine heart; and lean not unto thine own understanding.*
>
> *In all thy ways acknowledge him, and he shall direct thy paths.*
>
> (Proverbs 3:1-6)

The secret formula, the magic formula for life can be found in only one person, and that person is the Lord Jesus Christ.

Through Christ we have been given the indwelling presence of the Holy Spirit, and out of our innermost being shall flow His river of Living Water.

15

Our Strength and Our Defense

I believe without a doubt you would reply in the affirmative if I were to ask you, "Is Jesus Christ a person and are you conscious of personal fellowship with Him?"

If I were to ask you the same question about God the Father, you perhaps would say with a little less assurance that you feel He is a person even though you feel closer and more intimately associated with Jesus.

Finally, if I were to ask you if the Holy Spirit is a person and are you conscious of a personal relationship and a close communion and fellowship with Him, you would possibly answer, "I have never been really conscious of any personal fellowship with the Holy Spirit." You might even come back to me with a question and ask, "How is it possible for me to have a personal fellowship and communion with the Holy Spirit?"

Let us first of all examine several passages of Scripture that show us quite conclusively that the Holy Spirit is a person. Second, let us see that the Holy Spirit is God. Now we know that you cannot have fellowship with someone who is not a real person to you. Therefore, first of all we have to have proof from God's Word that the Holy Spirit is a person, and that the Holy Spirit is God.

Usually we divide the categories of personality into three realms: intellect, emotion, and will. With the intellect, a person can know, can think, and can understand. That is the reason I know that I am a person. You can be sure you are a person because you have intellect. Then there is the emotional capacity through which one can feel and can love.

Finally, there is the will by which a person can act and make decisions. You can prove that you are a person because you think, because you love, because you can put your will into action. And if we can see from the Word of God that the Holy Spirit has these capabilities, we would have to conclude that He is a person.

In 1 Corinthians 2:10 and 11, we have the ministry of the Holy Spirit that reveals His capacity of intellect. We read regarding the Holy Spirit: "God hath revealed them unto us by his Spirit: for the Spirit searcheth all things, yea, the deep things of God. For what man knoweth the things of a man, save the spirit of man which is in him? even so the things of God knoweth no man, but the Spirit of God."

Paul tells us here that the Spirit of God, the Holy Spirit, knows, and that He has intellect. Now what does the Spirit of God know? He knows the deep things of God, all that is in the Father; and all that is of divine truth that is in the Father is understood and is known by the Holy Spirit. Because He knows, He can reveal what He knows concerning God. He can reveal to us the deep secrets of the Father.

I cannot give you more than I have experienced myself. No man can teach something that he does not know himself, and one of the first requisites of a good teacher is that he must know his subject. Therefore, if the Holy Spirit is able to teach the things of Christ, if the Holy Spirit is able to reveal the things of the Father and the Son, it is because He knows the things of God, and the Spirit knows because He possesses the capacity of intellect. He has the ability to know, and that is one of the necessary components of a true personality.

Now let's look at Ephesians, Chapter 4, verse 30, where we have a clue to the emotional capacity of the Holy Spirit. "Grieve not the Holy Spirit of God, whereby ye are sealed unto the day of redemption." Now grief is a manifestation of the capacity of emotion, and a person must have the ability to love before love can be grieved. The fact that the Holy Spirit can be grieved is revelation that the Spirit possesses an emotional capacity that may be wounded by sins against His heart. That is one thing of which I am very careful. I am very sensitive to the Holy Spirit lest I grieve Him. You will never know what this Scripture means to me: "Grieve not the Holy Spirit of God." It is not in the sense that I fear His wrath. It is because I love Him, and I am so dependent upon Him that I would not grieve the Holy

Spirit of God for anything in the world. Paul understood that and that is the reason he gave us this command. He was showing us that the Holy Spirit possesses the capacity of emotion.

I learn so much every day of my life regarding this wonderful personality of the Holy Spirit. I believe that He has a sense of humor, and I think that is one of the reasons I enjoy the services so much. The Holy Spirit not only has the capacity for weeping, but for laughter and for joy and for peace. If you do not know the Holy Spirit in this capacity, you do not know what you have missed.

Now in 1 Corinthians 12, starting with verse 11, the Apostle Paul is teaching us about spiritual gifts and he writes, "But all these worketh that one and the selfsame Spirit, dividing to every man severally [individually] as He will." He tells us here that the distribution of spiritual gifts is a result of an act of the will of the Holy Spirit of God. Paul clearly attributes to the Holy Spirit the capacity of will.

When we put these three passages together, we observe that the Holy Spirit possesses the capacity of intellect so that He can know, the capacity of emotion so that He can love, and because He can be loved, His love can be sinned against.

Finally, He also has the capacity of will so that He can decide and bring action into being. Because of this, we would say that the Holy Spirit is not an influence. He is not a power emanating from God, nor a manifestation of God's personality.

The Holy Spirit is a person, such as you are a person, and the same proofs of His personality are demonstrated. We need never again think of the Holy Spirit in any other capacity than that of personality.

I have laid the ground work for something that is vitally important. If you are an individual (and you are), and a part

90

of humanity, you are fighting a three-fold enemy: the world, the flesh, and the devil. Because attacks are made against believers in the Lord Jesus Christ from one front, we have no right to assume that the enemy will always attack from that same front, and that we need not be on guard against the other avenues of invasion. The only defense against the enemy within, which is the flesh, is conscious dependence upon the Holy Spirit of God. The only defense that you and I have against the enticements of the world is conscious dependence upon the Holy Spirit.

There are some things that we must recognize. We find a very interesting fact about our adversary, the devil, in the Epistle of Jude, verse 9: "Yet Michael the archangel, when contending with the devil he disputed about the body of Moses, durst not bring against him [that is against the devil] a railing accusation, but said, The Lord rebuke thee."

Now this verse infers something of the power that belongs to Satan. I do not think you and I are always mindful of the power of Satan. There is only one power greater than the power of Satan, and that is the power of God. Michael, the archangel, did not have sufficient power of himself to argue with Satan. He had to call upon the power of God to defeat Satan in his desire to claim the body of Moses. If the archangel did not have power to stand against Satan, how can we expect to stand against him?

Satan possesses a supernatural power, a power above that which is possessed by men. He is an unseen adversary. He does not appear against us in the form of flesh and blood. The Apostle Paul wrote, "We wrestle not against flesh and blood" (Ephesians 6-12). If we were wrestling against another human, we would know the weak points of our adversary. But we are wrestling "against principalities, against powers, against the rulers of the darkness of this world, against spiritual wickedness in high places." Paul teaches that Satan has an organized system of which he is the head, and our adversary is always bent on destruction. That is the reason Peter writes, "Be sober, be vigilant: because your adversary the devil, as a roaring lion, walketh about, seeking whom he may devour" (1 Peter 5-8).

You may say that this paints a picture representing and depicting defeat. But it doesn't! No man, no woman need ever be defeated unless that one consents to defeat. Why? Here is the secret written in Isaiah 59:19: "When the enemy shall come in like a flood [when Satan, your adversary, the devil, comes in like a flood], the Spirit of the LORD [the Holy Spirit] shall lift up a standard against him."

That is proof positive that the Holy Spirit is a person. We must know the power and the personality of the mighty Third Person of the Trinity. He is more than an influence that is fighting in our behalf. He is not a mystery. There is a person, the Holy Spirit, and we need never go down in defeat. When the enemy shall come in like a flood, the Spirit of the LORD, the Holy Spirit, shall lift up a standard against him.

Perhaps now, my friend, you understand why I am so sold on the Holy Spirit. He is my defense and my strength, and He stands ready to be your defense and your strength as well!

16

Victory Through the Holy Spirit

There are only two forces in the world: the force of evil and the force of righteousness; and there is a mighty warfare that has gone on for generations—the war between God and Satan.

Once I was asked this question when I spoke before some young people: *Why did God make the devil?* My answer to them was this, God never made the devil.

Let me explain. In Isaiah 14, we see that Lucifer was once one of the most beautiful and wisest of all created beings. Angels, as you know, are created beings. Before God ever created man, He created legions of angels. In His creation of angels, He gave three angels—Michael, Gabriel, and Lucifer greater power than any of the other angels. Lucifer, in the Word of God, is called the Son of the Morning, and he was given a position of authority over one-third of all of the angels that God had created. One day it became evident that he was jealous of God, of His authority and power and worship. He said, "I will be like the Most High" (Isaiah 14:14), and he began to ascend into heaven to dethrone God. Thus, the first sins of which we have any record are the sins of jealousy and coveting.

Then something happened. In wrath, God threw Lucifer to the earth, not taking away from him his power, but leaving him a disembodied spirit. I have often wondered why God did not take away Lucifer's power but it is plain that He did not. Therefore, our adversary is no underling and no weakling. Our adversary, Satan or the devil, is a prince who has authority in his own realm. There is only one who has greater power than Satan, and that is God. It's no small thing when you contend with the devil. It's no small thing when you talk about Satan and his power.

In 2 Corinthians 4:4, Satan is referred to as the god of this world or this age. "In whom the god of this world hath blinded the minds of them which believe not, lest the light of the glorious gospel of Christ, who is the image of God, should shine unto them."

Have you ever wondered why that member of your family or that neighbor or friend is unable to see spiritual things? Here is your answer. "In whom the god of this world [Satan] hath blinded the minds of them which believe not." Satan does not want you or any human being to believe in God. Therefore, he has the power to literally "blind the minds of them which believe not, lest the light of the glorious gospel of Christ, who is the image of God, should shine unto them."

Satan has elevated himself to a position of prominence, not only in governments, but in religious spheres as well. He claims the worship that belongs to God Almighty, and he causes men, through delusion in false religious systems, to worship him. He doesn't care how religious you are. In fact, he wants you to be religious—but there is a great difference between being religious and being a *born-again* Christian. It's significant that those who worship Satan do not necessarily become irreligious nor do they become enemies of religion. You don't have to become an enemy of religion or be irreligious to be controlled by Satan and to be lost.

You see, that's the reason, in speaking of these last days—and these are surely the closing hours of this dispensation—prophecy is being fulfilled every hour of the day. But the Spirit of God warned us that in these last days we should be careful of strong delusions and falseness in religion. It's one thing to speak of Jesus, but it's another thing to accept Him as the very Son of the Living God. Satan does not care if you talk about Jesus. Satan would love it if every man, woman, and young person would look to Jesus as a wonderful example of a mere man, and see Him only as the greatest of men that ever lived. He doesn't mind that at all. But he does care when one accepts the Son of the Living God as his personal Savior. That's what makes all the difference in the world.

What I am saying here is something that is very important. You may become a devotee of a religious system, but if it doesn't center on the Lord Jesus Christ, nor recognize the sovereign authority of the Almighty God, it's a religious system that centers in Satan's counterfeit. Thus Satan may truly be called the god of this world. He always operates by deception. Jesus said that Satan is a liar and the father of lies (John 8:44). As such, Satan will never operate according to truths. He knows no such thing as truth. His very nature is one of deception, and there is great deception in the world today.

Remember, the Lord Jesus Christ is *the Way, the Truth, and the Life* (John 14:6). Truth centers in a person, and that person is Jesus Christ the Son of God. Truth is revealed from God to man through Jesus Christ, who is truth. Satan operates in a sphere that is totally different from the sphere of God. Since God always operates in the truth, Satan operates in the opposite of truth, in the sphere of lies and deception. Satan is a liar. Satan is a deceiver. And Paul says that Satan operates by blinding the minds of men.

You see, the mind is the faculty that receives truth and assimilates truth. Now if Satan would perpetrate a lie, he must first of all darken the perceptive powers of men so that they don't recognize his deception. If you knew that he was the deceiver of the truth, then you would be on guard. But first of all he must blind your mind to the fact that he is the great deceiver, so that you don't recognize the fact of his deception. Therefore, he must first of all transform himself into an angel of light to deceive men into believing that he presents the truth, when he is actually presenting a lie. Now this is borne out in passages such as Revelation 20:2-3 where the angel laid hold of "the dragon, that old serpent, which is the Devil, and Satan, and bound him a thousand years, and cast him into the bottomless pit, and shut him up, and set a seal upon him, that he should deceive the nations no more."

The thing that characterizes the work of Satan in this world is that he deceives the nations, and he is still deceiving mankind to this very hour. His is a ministry of deception and blindness to the truth. *Jesus Christ is the truth*. The blindness among the nations, among the rulers of the nations, and the leaders of nations is appalling. Many have followed the prince of the power of the air, have become enslaved in his system so that his deception has become their philosophy The very atmosphere today is filled with great deception, and the minds of men, clothed in this great deception, do not begin to realize the great power of the enemy over their minds and bodies. The enemy *never* practices truth. He is *always* the great deceiver.

In Ephesians 6:11, the Apostle is referring to this fact when he points out that we are to "Put on the whole armor of God, that ye may be able to stand against the wiles of the devil." In his day, Paul knew without question the kind of things I'm talking about. He's the one who warned us, and it was the Holy Spirit who gave Paul this great revelation. Paul contended with the devil, and came face to face with Satan and his power over and over again. Thus the Holy Spirit through Paul points out that you and I are to put on the whole armor of God so that we may be able to stand against the wiles of the devil.

We don't expect that Satan will burst upon us with a formal and open attack. He is too crafty and subtle for that. Our enemy is not one whose movements we can predict nor can we know exactly what he will do because he appears to conform to truth. A thing may look so harmless to us. The beginnings may appear very innocent, but the thing grows. Talk to any young person who was caught in the snare of drugs and they will admit it all began innocently.

Listen to me right now. The enemy is an enemy who rules by deception and deceit. He does not appear against us in flesh and blood and that is why the Apostle said, "we wrestle not against flesh and blood" (Ephesians 6:12). If we were wrestling against another human being we would know the weak points in our adversary and therefore know where to strike.

But my friend, *I have good news for you.* There is still victory for any man and any woman. You need only to *take* the victory, and that victory is found in Jesus Christ, the Son of the Living God. That's the reason you and I need the power of God, for only *one* power and *one* person is greater than the power of Satan. That power is the power of the Lord Jesus Christ through the person of the Holy Spirit. You do not have to be defeated on a single score if you have accepted Christ as your Savior, for you and I "are more than conquerors through him [Christ] that loved us" (Romans 8:37).

The Seal of the
Holy Spirit

17

Born Again

$\mathcal{S}$ometimes I wonder if many Christians fully appreciate and realize the believer's place in the Body of Christ. In fact, I have wondered if *I* fully appreciate and realize and have any concept of what is my full inheritance in Christ Jesus. With this thought in mind, let's look at Ephesians 1:3-14:

Blessed be the God and Father of our Lord Jesus Christ, who hath blessed us with all spiritual blessings in heavenly places in Christ:

According as he hath chosen us in him before the foundation of the world, that we should be holy and without blame before Him in love:

Having predestinated us unto the adoption of children by Jesus Christ to himself, according to the good pleasure of his will,

To the praise of the glory of his grace, wherein he hath made us accepted in the beloved.

In whom we have redemption through his blood, the forgiveness of sins, according to the riches of his grace;

Wherein he hath abounded toward us in all wisdom and prudence;

Having made known unto us the mystery of his will, according to his good pleasure which he hath purposed in himself:

That in the dispensation of the fullness of times he might gather together in one all things in Christ, both which are in heaven, and which are on earth; even in him:

In whom also we have obtained an inheritance, being predestinated according to the purpose of him who worketh all things after the counsel of his own will:

That we should be to the praise of his glory, who first trusted in Christ.

In whom ye also trusted, after that ye heard the word of truth, the gospel of your salvation: in whom also after that ye believed, ye were sealed with that holy Spirit of promise,

Which is the earnest of our inheritance until the redemption of the purchased possession, unto the praise of his glory.

Perhaps you have read this portion of the Word of God many times, but whenever you have come to this part of the Scriptures, "in whom also after that ye believed, ye were sealed with that holy Spirit of promise," you may not have fully realized or understood what is actually meant by the sealing with the Holy Spirit.

In this portion of the Word of God, the word "predestinated" appears several times. The Scripture clearly teaches that every human being, from the first Adam to the last one who will ever be born in the flesh, was in the beginning predestined in the mind of God, in the plan of God, and in the heart of God to be His heir and a joint-heir with His only begotten Son. In other words, every human being in the mind of God was predestined to be born again. But all human beings are not Christians. All are not born again. The Scripture clearly teaches, "God is not willing that any should perish" (2 Peter 3:9). God has not willed that any human being should be lost. God never willed that you should be a sinner. God never willed that you should go to hell. Hell was never made for humanity. Hell was made for fallen angels, and never made for mankind.

But watch. Man was created with free moral agency. I was not forced to say or do what I am doing. I could have chosen many other professions in the world other than that which I am doing, and God knows that almost anything that I might have chosen of myself may have been easier, but I am doing this by choice.

Yes, by choice I am doing what I am doing. By choice I am a Christian. No one forced me to be a Christian. My father never forced me. My mother never forced me. No power forced me to be a Christian, to choose the Christ as my personal Savior, to walk this life as a Christian. I was born with free moral agency, and a will of my own, a will separate and apart from the will of anyone else in the world, a will separate and apart from even God Himself. In exactly the same way Jesus had a will separate and apart from the will of the Father when He walked this earth and was as much man as though He were not God.

Then the day came when I had a choice to make, and I chose to be a Christian. That Sunday morning in that little Methodist Church in Concordia, Missouri, no one asked me, no one urged or put pressure on me. Few people who were gathered in that church that day knew what it meant to be "born again." But in that moment, the Holy Spirit spoke to my heart, and as a young girl almost 14 years of age, I saw myself a sinner. I saw Jesus as a Savior for my sins, and I made the choice, the greatest and wisest choice that I have ever made in my entire life. I exercised my will and I chose Jesus as my Savior. I made that choice, not for a day, not for six months, but forever.

God is not willing that I should perish or be lost, and in exactly the same way God is not willing that you should perish. Every individual has to make his own choice, and there is not a person in hell—there will never be a person in hell—who can point a finger at Almighty God and say, "You chose to put me here. I am here because You made the choice for me." No, beloved. It is God's will that you be born again. He has predestined that you be born again, but you and I make our own lives. We must make our own choices: to either accept the pardon or reject the pardon.

Think a minute. That is exactly what it is—a pardon. When Jesus died on the Cross and cried, "It is finished," a pardon was perfected for all humanity. All on earth that you have to do is accept that pardon. The Holy Spirit is the convicting power of the Trinity. He is the one who shows you that you are a sinner. That is His work. Then the very minute that you accept that pardon, something happens.

When we are born again, something wonderful happens. Explain it? I do not believe there is a single Christian living this very hour who has words in his or her vocabulary to fully express or describe what happened at that time of conversion. You cannot do it. I do not believe that it is possible because it is of the Spirit. "That which is born of the flesh is flesh; and that which is born of the Spirit is spirit" (John 3:6). That is the reason that John, in the Book of the Revelation, had such a difficult time trying to describe what he saw in the spirit, because it is a different vocabulary entirely. You cannot describe your spiritual experiences. You cannot describe to anyone else that which you experienced in being born again, or that experience that you had of being filled with the Spirit. But each is a definite transaction, and in that moment it is something more than passing from death unto life, it is something more than just having your past covered with the blood, it is something more than the forgiveness of one's sins. Up until that time, God had been your mighty Creator, but in accepting Christ as your Savior, God became your Heavenly Father. He does not become our Heavenly Father until after we have accepted Jesus Christ His Son as our Savior, and only then are we adopted by Him.

Oh, this is glorious! "Behold, what manner of love the Father hath bestowed upon us that we should be called children of God," and such we are, because we have been adopted by the Father. But He does not adopt us until we accept His Son in the forgiveness of our sins, then for the very first time we become a part of the family of God. And that is what it is, we are born into this Family of God.

18

Wanted by God

That wonderful born-again experience is just the beginning of a new life, and sometimes I think that few of us realize our full inheritance as one of the King's children, and that is exactly what we are. It grieves me that some of God's children live such defeated lives. We can give the unregenerated, the unsaved man or woman, the wrong impression and the wrong idea about God's children. We are heirs of God, and do you know what that means? If you are a born-again Christian, you are literally a joint-heir with Christ, and that comes from the highest authority in heaven and earth. That is what God's Word assures: we are heirs of God if we are born again.

Ephesians 1:12 reads, "That we should be to the praise of his glory, who first trusted in Christ." We talk about faith, and we dwell so much on our faith in Him, but there was never greater faith than the faith that God the Father had in Jesus Christ when He sent Him to pay the price of our salvation. First, God trusted in Him. That is the real example of faith, and God gave us that example. Verses 13-14 continue, "In whom ye also trusted, after that ye heard the word of truth, the gospel of your salvation: in whom also after that ye believed, ye were sealed with that Holy Spirit of promise, Which is the earnest of our inheritance until the redemption of the purchased possession, unto the praise of his glory."

Here we are going to focus our attention on this wonderful seal of the Holy Spirit, "after that ye believed." First of all, there must be that transaction of having accepted the pardon—by faith accepting that which Jesus did on the Cross. At that moment, God the Father becomes your Heavenly Father. Then something else happens, which you have heard me say over and over again: *I pray that His Spirit shall bear witness with your spirit that you have passed from death unto life.* What is it? At that moment when you accept Christ as your Savior, all three persons of the Trinity are active. The moment that you accept that which Jesus has done for you in the forgiveness of your sins, accepting Him as your Personal Savior, God the Creator becomes your Heavenly Father, and you are adopted of Him into this great family of God, born into the Body of Christ.

At the same time, the Holy Spirit places His seal upon the individual, confirming the transaction—the Seal of the Spirit. "After that ye believed, ye were sealed with that holy

Spirit of promise," and that is exactly what the Scripture means when His Spirit bears witness with our spirit. How do we know that we have been born again? We cannot explain it for there are no words in our vocabulary to describe our experience, and that is the reason the skeptic, the unbeliever, cannot understand. But at that moment, when the Holy Spirit puts the seal upon the transaction, His Spirit (the Holy Spirit) bears witness with our spirit that we have passed from death unto life, that we have been adopted by the Father, born into the Body of Christ—and *we know that we know that we know!*

Now pause a minute. This thing of the believer in the Body of Christ, as an heir of God, means much more than most of us realize. Stop and consider the Heavenly Father's loving acts toward His children who are born again, to those who are a part of the family of God. First of all, let us consider the loving Heavenly Father's part. God has blessed us in Christ with all blessings, and I often wonder if we fully realize that you and I are only blessed as He blesses us. There are times that we feel so independent, so self-sufficient, and then in awe of our self-sufficiency we get ourselves into serious trouble. Some of the smartest people I know can get themselves into the most stupid messes because they are using their own wisdom. It is like trying to bless themselves. But you and I are only blessed as He blesses. God has blessed us in Christ with all blessings, and with His blessings we are the richest persons in the world. He has chosen us in His love before all time.

Let me make another comparison here, using Joe Kuhlman, who is my earthly father, my Papa. It is the nicest thing and the greatest feeling in the world when children know that they are wanted. I know I was not an unwanted child because Papa and Mama wanted me. All through life that is something that I have kept inside of me and treasured. It has made me feel good, like a hidden jewel. But we are all well aware that there are thousands and thousands of children living today, walking the streets, who were not wanted. But everyone of God's children was wanted. He has chosen us in His love before all time. You may have been an unwanted child when it came to your earthly parents, but there is a Heavenly Father who has wanted you before you saw the light of day. Even before the foundation of the world, you were wanted and loved by Him. He has predestined us in His good pleasure to the place of His children and enriched us in His grace with an abundant endowment.

On the other hand, in your earthly family you could have been wanted and yet sometimes there wasn't enough meat for everyone to have a portion. Winter came and though your Dad loved you, there wasn't enough money to buy you the shoes that you needed for your feet. He loved you but love had nothing to do with it. He was working hard, but we are still in an old material world. You can be loved, you can be wanted, and yet be poor so far as material things are concerned. Do you want to know something about the Heavenly Father? You are one of His children, a part of His family, born again when you accepted His Son, and He has enriched you in His grace with an abundant endowment. None of His children are poor.

Sometimes I think we have the wrong sense of values and we need to come back again to a true sense of values. If you have peace of mind, you are rich. If you can lie down at night and put your head on that pillow and go to sleep with peace of mind and peace of soul, you have something that some of the richest men in the whole world know nothing about. If you can know and have the assurance that underneath all of the uncertainties of life you have a sure refuge in Christ, you have security. In this day and age, if you have security in God, you are rich. God's security does not last for a day, or the next six months. God's security reaches throughout all eternity. He has enriched us with an abundant endowment, He has revealed to us His great secret as to His plan. He has displayed in us His glory in the action of His love, sealed us with His Spirit, thus marking us as His own possession.

If you have had this wonderful experience of being born again, you have God's mark upon you. He has sealed you with His Spirit, thus marking you as His own possession. *You are rich!*

19

Our Inheritance in Christ

*N*o man or woman need ever be defeated. You do not need to go down in defeat. It does not matter under what circumstances you are living. You were not made for defeat. You are only defeated when you consent to defeat. You have One at the right hand of God the Father, in position of great High Priest, the Son of the Living God, our Great Advocate, who ever lives to make intercession for you. In this moment I pray that He will give you divine hope, that great spiritual hope, and victory in Jesus' Name.

As I continue to discuss with you this "Sealing of the Holy Spirit," perhaps you have wondered what Paul really meant in that first chapter of Ephesians, verse thirteen: "In whom ye also trusted, after that ye heard the word of truth, the gospel of your salvation; . . ." That is what the Word of truth is—the Gospel of your Salvation!

Then he continues: ". . . in whom also after that ye believed . . . ." It did not happen when you first heard the Word of truth, nor before you were born again. Let me explain something here and give you the setting. You heard the Word of truth and the Holy Spirit convicted you. That truth was the gospel of your salvation and then, after you believed and you accepted the truth, after you accepted Jesus Christ as your Savior, you were sealed with that Holy Spirit of promise, "which is the earnest of our inheritance until the redemption of the purchased possession, unto the praise of his glory."

Here and now, living in these bodies of flesh, you and I are receiving only an earnest, a down payment, of our inheritance in Christ. If you are God's child, you belong to Him, you have been adopted of the Father, and all these wonderful things are yours: peace of mind, peace of soul, His love, His blessings, His goodness, this wonderful joy that He gives to His children, and this assurance He is with you underneath all the uncertainties of life. No matter what your spiritual experience may have been, God has much more in store for you.

You may have felt that you stood on Pisgah's lofty mountain top, or you may have come out from a glorious service and said, "Dear Lord, turn it off. I cannot take any more. This is too wonderful." Yet, no matter what your experiences may have been or what you may have at this moment, that which you have experienced is still only an earnest, a down payment. Your redemption and mine will not be perfected until we stand in God's glorious presence, when that which is mortal will put on immortality.

How can anything be absolute perfection or the ultimate so long as we are in these physical bodies, these bodies that are still corruption and mortal? There is pain, there is suffering and old age. There are problems in this life and heartaches and tears. Therefore, this cannot be the ultimate, this cannot be perfection. These things that I am talking to you about, this peace of mind, this security, this joy, this wonderful assurance of knowing that we belong to Christ is only an earnest. But one of these days when this which is mortal will have put on incorruption, there will be no more tears, no more problems, no troubles or suffering or temptations. Today we see by faith. Tomorrow our redemption will have been perfected when we see Him face to face, garbed in bodies like unto His.

Now let us look at this portion of Scripture again in that light. Paul is talking to the believers: "After that you heard the word of truth, the gospel of your salvation: in whom also after that you believed, you were sealed with that Holy Spirit of promise, which is the earnest of our inheritance until the redemption of the purchased possession, unto the praise of his glory." Our glorious future has been bought and paid for, and there is no mortgage against it. No matter what happens to interest down here on earth, or what happens to the stock markets, that which is our inheritance in Christ has been bought and paid for. It is a purchased possession.

As a result, there is no need for any Christian to live a defeated life. If you have been living like a pauper, acting like a pauper, and feeling like a pauper, maybe you don't know who you really are. You are rich! If you have been born again, then God is your Heavenly Father. You have been adopted of Him, and the Holy Spirit has placed His seal upon that transaction. You were sealed with that Holy Spirit of promise; therefore, His Spirit bears witness with your spirit that you have passed from death unto life.

Let me add this for good measure as you bring back to mind these facts: you have the Father, the Son and the Holy Spirit—each with a separate and distinct work in dealing with you as God's adopted child. Remember that the Father is the source of every blessing, the giver of every good and perfect gift. Jesus His Son is the channel through which all things are given and the channel by which we have eternal life. Always and at all times, Jesus remains the channel through which these things are given. But remember: the Father is the source of every blessing, the giver of every good and perfect gift.

Now we come to the Holy Spirit, who is the power of the Trinity. Yes, the Father is the source of every blessing, and perhaps you have also known that Jesus made all things possible to us, but it is the Holy Spirit who is the power. That is why people are healed sitting in their seats at the miracle services. You do not need me to lay hands on you. When the Holy Spirit is present, the power of the Trinity, His very presence will heal a sick body as that one sits in His presence. That is His power!

Now remember something: believers and believers only are sealed with the Holy Spirit of promise. God owns us. We are His adopted children with the right to all privileges and inheritance as His children. "Behold, what manner of love the Father hath bestowed upon us, that we should be called the sons of God" (1 John 3: 1). We have received the Spirit of adoption, and the Spirit Himself bears witness with our spirit that we are the children of God. We are sealed because of what we are in Him, not because of any merit of our own. We are sealed because of that which Jesus did, and the Holy Spirit Himself seals that transaction.

Now what is the seal? It is not some emotion, and please let me make that perfectly clear lest you labor under a false illusion. No, it is not some emotion, but *the presence of the Holy Spirit* in the believer witnessing to his full acceptance in Christ. In 1 John 4:17, the Apostle says, "As he is, so are we in this world," heirs of God and joint heirs with Christ Jesus. Let me urge you again: *Never forget to Whom you belong!*

20

The Holy Spirit Can Be Grieved

We are going to go a little deeper in this study of the person of the Holy Spirit, and you are going to see a different side of Him than perhaps you have ever seen before: His sensitivity. It is one of the reasons He is likened to a dove, the gentlest of all birds.

It is wonderful when you see Him in His strength, the mighty power of the Trinity, and to know that He defends us. Then when we realize that you and I can have fellowship and this wonderful communion with Him, it is almost beyond our comprehension. Next, we realize that He is our great teacher regarding spiritual things, the great revealer of all truth. But I want you to know there is another side to this personality, and that is that He can be grieved.

There is a Scripture in this connection, but since we dare not take God's Word out of its setting, let us begin with Ephesians 4:1-2: "I therefore, the prisoner of the Lord, beseech you that ye walk worthy of the vocation wherewith ye are called, with all lowliness and meekness, with longsuffering, forbearing one another in love."

I pause here because these fruits of the Spirit are so lacking in many Christian lives and in the Church today. The sin of jealousy is often present even in the lives of those who profess to be filled with the Spirit. Many do not know what meekness means today. Humility, one of the greatest of all Christian graces, is lacking, and we see so much spiritual bigotry on every hand and little lowliness, meekness, longsuffering, and love.

Let us read the next verse, Ephesians 4:3— "Endeavoring to keep the unity of the Spirit in the bond of peace." It means something to be born again. It means something to follow in the footsteps of Jesus, to take up our cross and follow Him. As surely as there was a Cross for Jesus and a death on that Cross, so surely is there a cross for everyone who has been born again. There must be death to *self* if we are to follow Him in the spirit of lowliness, meekness, and longsuffering; forbearing one another in love, and endeavoring to keep the unity of the Spirit in the bond of peace.

"There is one body, and one Spirit [the Holy Spirit], even as ye are called in one hope of your calling, one Lord, one faith, one baptism" (Ephesians 4:4-5). You may ask the question: Which is the *real* church? We have thousands of organizations and you will find a church on many corners of some cities. These are organizations. But only the Lord Jesus Christ can say, "My Church." It is wonderful that we have these organizations where we can fellowship with other Christians, but when it comes to *the* Church, it is the Body of Christ. We are born into His body, and born into His Church.

Let us see what baptism Paul is talking about in that 5th verse. It is the same baptism that is referred to in 1 Corinthians 12:12-13. Remember, you cannot take something out of its context and make a doctrine out of it, and here we have the answer to what baptism he's referring to. "For as the body is one, and hath many members, and all the members of that one body, being many, are one body: so also is Christ. *For by one Spirit are we all baptized into one* body, whether we be Jews or Gentiles, whether we be bond or free; and have been all made to drink into one Spirit" (italics added). That is the same baptism, the same Body of Christ that is referred to here in the 4th chapter of Ephesians: "one Lord, one faith, one baptism, one God and Father of all, who is above all, and through all, and in you all" (verses 5 and 6).

Now let us go to Ephesians 4:26-32, which I referred to at the start of this message:

Be ye angry, and sin not: let not the sun go down upon your wrath:

Neither give place to the devil.

Let him that stole steal no more: but rather let him labor, working with his hands the thing which is good, that he may have to give to him that needeth.

Let no corrupt communication proceed out of your mouth, but that which is good to the use of edifying, that it may minister grace unto the hearers.

And grieve not the Holy Spirit of God, whereby ye are sealed unto the day of redemption.

Let all bitterness, and wrath, and anger, and clamour, and evil speaking, be put away from you, with all malice:

And be ye kind one to another, tenderhearted, forgiving one another, even as God for Christ's sake hath forgiven you.

We are cautioned lest we grieve the Holy Spirit. How can one grieve the Holy Spirit? Keep in mind that even though the Holy Spirit is the mighty power of the Trinity, He is sensitive and easily grieved. There is no doubt that this wonderful person may be grieved by bitterness, by wrath, anger, evil speaking. In other words, He can be grieved by anything in the life of an individual that is contrary to meekness, longsuffering, forbearing one another in love, and endeavoring to keep the unity of the Spirit in the bond of peace. Anything contrary to these things will grieve the Holy Spirit.

I still contend that it is not what you profess or what spiritual experiences you may have had in the past. If there is an unforgiving spirit within you, if there is malice, if there is an evil tongue, if there is jealousy in your heart, if there is somebody against whom you are holding a grudge, if you are a gossip, if you lie, then the Holy Spirit will not dwell in your vessel. He cannot, because these things are contrary to His personality. Under these conditions, the Holy Spirit cannot and will not make that body of yours His temple. Why? Because these things are sin and they grieve the Holy Spirit. He cannot and will not abide in the same vessel with sin.

We are going to see something here about the Holy Spirit. There are those who have been so concerned about that sin for which there is no forgiveness—the unpardonable sin. The Bible speaks of it as the only sin for which there is no forgiveness, neither in this world, or in the world to come. There are many ideas regarding this sin but this, too, must not be taken out of its context that we might understand it rightly.

Read Matthew 12:22-30:

Then was brought unto him [Jesus] one possessed with a devil, blind, and dumb; and he healed him [it is Jesus doing the healing*], insomuch that the blind and dumb both spake and saw.*

And all the people were amazed, and said, Is not this the son of David [referring to Jesus]?

But when the Pharisees heard it, they said, This fellow doth not cast out devils, but by Beelzebub the prince of the devils [they called Jesus a devil].

And Jesus knew their thoughts, and said unto them, Every kingdom divided against itself is brought to desolation: and every city or house divided against itself shall not stand:

And if Satan cast out Satan, he is divided against himself; how shall then his kingdom stand?

And if I by Beelzebub cast out devils, by whom do your children cast them out? therefore, they shall be your judges.

> *But if I cast out devils by the Spirit of God, then
> the kingdom of God is come unto you.*
>
> *Or else how can one enter into a strong man's
> house, and spoil his goods, except he first bind the
> strong man? And then he will spoil his house.*
>
> *He that is not with me is against me; and he that
> gathereth not with me scattereth abroad.*

Now this is what follows in the same connection. What
the Pharisees were doing was attributing the work of God
and the Holy Spirit to the devil. The Holy Spirit through
Jesus had just cast out the devil and one who had been
blind and dumb had been healed—"and the blind and dumb
both spake and saw." The Pharisees said, That is the work
of the devil, of Satan. Jesus replied, How can Satan cast
out Satan? He would be working against himself.

In the light of that context, read this:

> *Wherefore I say unto you, All manner of sin and
> blasphemy shall be forgiven unto men: but the
> blasphemy against the Holy Ghost shall not be
> forgiven unto men.*
>
> *And whosoever speaketh a word against the Son
> of man, it shall be forgiven him: but whosoever
> speaketh against the Holy Ghost, it shall not be
> forgiven him, neither in this world, neither in the
> world to come (Matthew 12:31-32).*

There is one sin for which there is no pardon, and that
is the sin of blasphemy against the Holy Ghost. The gifts of
the Holy Ghost manifested through the apostles, and the
power of God displayed in the lives of individuals, were the

last proof that God designed for the confirmation of the gospel. They are still kept in reserve and in evidence today. When a man or woman attributes the work of the Holy Spirit to the work of Satan, that one commits the sin for which there is no forgiveness, either in this world or in the world to come.

Be careful what you say regarding the work of the Holy Ghost lest you commit the sin for which there is no forgiveness.

21

Our Wills Under the Control of the Holy Spirit

*T*hese are such exciting days for God's children, the days that the Scripture refers to when it says, "When these things begin to come to pass, then look up, lift up your heads; for your redemption draweth nigh" (Luke 21:28). This is the hour when again the fruits and the gifts of the Spirit are all being restored to the church. This is a great hour of restoration so far as the things of the Spirit are concerned. I know it is getting dark out there for the unbeliever, darker with every passing hour, but our future is so bright, so glorious. Our redemption is drawing nigh and, remember, our redemption will not be perfected as Christians and heirs of God and joint heirs with Christ Jesus until we see Him face to face. This is the hour when literally thousands are being filled with the Holy Spirit—that wonderful experience that we call the Baptism with the Holy Spirit.

I want, therefore, to talk to you about something that is vitally important in relationship to the Baptism of the Holy Spirit and its significance for our wills. This is something that is often overlooked, and it is important that we realize that our wills—your will, my will—can be separate and apart from the will of God and how it relates to this wonderful experience and to the person of the Holy Spirit and to Himself.

Hebrews 10:16 says, "This is the covenant that I will make with them after those days, saith the Lord, I will put my laws into their hearts, and in their minds will I write them."

Because the Baptism of the Spirit affects our emotional life, we must not forget that the most important part of this experience affects that which is not always visible, and that is our wills. We must be careful that we do not misinterpret or accept some great emotional experience for the Baptism of the Holy Spirit. Sometimes I think that we are so human that we get carried away by some great emotional experience and then label it as the Baptism of the Holy Spirit.

The root is the most important part of any tree. No man will take issue with that statement, and the most important part of our spiritual life is that which cannot be seen with the eyes of men. The most important part of my life is my will. The most important part of your life is your will. When it comes to your spiritual experience, your relationship to God, to Jesus Christ, and to the Holy Spirit, it is your will that is most important. Sometimes our will is one thing that we like to talk about and discuss the least. But when it comes to the place where we can honestly say, "Nevertheless, not my will but thine be done," we come to the place that very few people know.

Reading the Word and carefully noting its translation to practical living, we must arrive at the conclusion that the most important part of all points in this experience is that the Holy Spirit gets full control of our will. There are thousands who profess to the experience of being filled with the Holy Spirit; yet they know absolutely nothing in that experience of giving the Holy Spirit full control of their will. It is not what happens at that moment of the Baptism of the Holy Spirit, but it is what happens following that experience. If the Holy Spirit does not have full control of your will, the experience will be shallow and passing. It is possible for those who are not deeply spiritual to be so gripped by a powerful spiritual meeting, that they are drawn into the movement of enthusiasm without having their very nature changed.

When God revealed Himself at Mizpah in the days of Saul, some of the men following after Saul in their quest to capture David were gripped by the same spirit of ecstasy that swayed the prophets. It is possible to be in attendance at a powerful spiritual prayer meeting, to receive a wonderful experience, but still miss the deep and abiding blessing. This abiding blessing comes only as the Spirit is permitted to go to the depth of our being and change the root of our lives. Your mind and will must be under the absolute control of the Spirit if the blessing and the experience are to abide.

This is a teaching that is very practical and needed today. I am not speaking of merely a great emotional

129

experience. I am talking about an experience that grips and changes your mind. It is a spiritual experience when you literally surrender not only your mind, but your will to the will of God. It is something that is not just temporary but something that will be with you when the waters are deep and about to overflow, and when the night is so dark there isn't a star in your sky. Troubles and tribulations and testing times come. You are secure, however, even while your tears are blinding you and you're unable to fully understand, but you're saying: "Nevertheless, not my will, but Thine be done!"

The real foundation to our mind and its makeup is the will. After all these years in the ministry, I have observed that it is of utmost importance that our will be under the control of the Spirit of God. You may boast of having been filled with the Spirit and having received the Baptism with the Holy Spirit, but let me ask you something: *Is that will of yours today under the control of the Holy Spirit?* If it is not, then I would not give you much for whatever experience you had. It was only something that was temporary. If God is given our wills to rule, then He will have our entire life under His control.

When the Holy Spirit comes upon an individual, and God conquers the will and becomes the supreme power in that life, then the whole life for all time is affected by this experience. From then on the individual no longer has the final word in life, but the Holy Spirit is the one who controls that life. The Scriptures call this, *crucifixion*. The will of man is set aside and gives place to the will of God. It is then that one can say and know: I have found my life, for I lost my will to God's will.

My Prayer for You

*F*ather, this thing of living a Christian life is the greatest thing, the most practical thing in the world. It is the only life, and if we can only learn how to live, if we can only live according to Your laws, if we can only be honest with ourselves and honest with You, there is no limit to what You will do for every man and every woman.

How often we have defeated Your plan for us. There isn't a single Christian who has not been guilty of defeating Your plan some place along the line. I know I have been guilty more than once because of my own imperfections, because of what is termed "little sins." We know it is the little termites that can cause a big building to tumble, those tiny termites that eat and eat away until finally there is total destruction. In the same way, it is those "little sins" that eat at our hearts, that destroy Your purpose for our lives, that rob us of something that we might have been and might have done for You.

I pray in the name of Jesus the Son of the Living God, that You will destroy any termites of sin in our lives. Cleanse us of all of them as we look ourselves directly in the face and confess our own sins and shortcomings. Search our hearts, O Lord.

In Jesus' name and for Jesus' sake, destroy the termites. Help us to keep our eyes off self and on You. Give us vision and take us out of ourselves. Father, I pray for a fresh baptism of Your love and an honesty that we have never had before. And above everything else, keep us where the Holy Spirit can use us, that the most profitable days of our lives shall be from this day forward, for time is running out. Our responsibility is great. May not one of us fail You, and in all things may the world see Jesus and Jesus only in us.

Amen

Questions Regarding the Holy Spirit

*R*arely a day passes that I don't receive questions about the Holy Spirit and the work of this Third Person of the Trinity. So I am going to answer some of these questions that I believe may have been on your heart, too.

1. Will God take His Spirit out of the world when the Church is raptured?

First of all, let me explain something in answering this question. When we refer to the rapture of the Church, we refer to the time when the Holy Spirit leaves this earth. He is literally the rapture power, the power of the great *catching up*. Those who are alive and who will have a part in the rapture of the Church will go up with the Holy Spirit.

We know that when Jesus left this old world, standing there on the Mount of Olives, He went alone. Those who were near Him, near enough to see Him go, did not leave with Him. They stood there and watched Him leave. When He went, He went alone. But, as surely as Jesus left this earth and went back to the Father, so surely is the day coming when the Holy Spirit will leave in exactly the same manner. When the Holy Spirit goes, however, He does not go alone. He takes the Bride of Christ, the Church, with Him. If you have been born into the Body of Christ, having had that new birth experience, living that victorious Christian life in Christ Jesus—if you are a part of this glorious, victorious, body—then you are a part of the Bride of Christ. Therefore, in that moment when the Holy Spirit's work is finished on this earth and He leaves, He will take you and all born-again believers along with Him. That in reality is what the rapture of the Church is.

2. Can anyone who has had the knowledge of the Lord Jesus Christ be saved after the rapture when the Holy Spirit has been taken out of the earth?

Before Jesus went away He clearly told of the great work of the Holy Spirit to be carried out while He is here on the earth. "When he is come, he will reprove the world of sin, and of righteousness, and of judgment: of sin, because they believe not on me; of righteousness, because I go to my Father, and ye see me no more; of judgment, because the prince of this world is judged" (John 16: 8-11).

In other words, the Holy Spirit is the mighty convicting power. If you have known any conviction whatsoever, it is the Holy Spirit who has convicted you. Do you remember that convicting power? You may not have been aware of that which was really happening, but you rolled and tossed all night long and could not sleep. It was the Holy Spirit speaking to your heart. Do you remember the very first time you realized you were a sinner and needed to be born again? It was the convicting power of the Holy Spirit who revealed this to you. But when the Holy Spirit has been taken out of the earth, man will no longer know His convicting power.

3. Will there be any saved during the seven years of the great tribulation upon the earth, after the Holy Spirit is gone?

My answer is, *indeed yes!* Now I have already said that there will no longer be the convicting power of the Holy Spirit to make those here on earth aware of their sins, but it will be possible for them to be saved through the knowledge of the Word of God.

I have prepared hundreds and hundreds of thirty-minute tapes on the Word of God. I tried to cover as much of God's Word as I possibly could on those tapes. You may wonder why and my answer is simply this: So that after the rapture of the Church, after I am gone and all of God's children have been taken up out of the earth, the Word of God can still go forth and many a man or woman who did not listen to me before, who had no regard whatsoever for the Word of God, will listen then. They will be glad to listen. There is coming the day when they will see that these things that I'm talking about now are real. Hearing the Word, without any convicting power of the Holy Spirit, they will accept the Word, and when they accept the Word, they will accept Jesus Christ on facts, not because of any conviction. Thus there will be thousands and thousands saved in this way during the tribulation period.

4. Were the Old Testament prophets filled with the Holy Spirit—in other words, were these prophets baptized with the Spirit before the Day of Pentecost?

You may recall that I dealt with this question in part earlier, but I'll touch on this subject again briefly. You will possibly remember something I said before: when the Old Testament saints were filled with the Holy Spirit, it was a sovereign act of God. The Holy Spirit was not a gift to all the Old Testament saints. Today, being filled with the Holy Spirit is a gift that Jesus left to His Church. It is the perfect will of Jesus and our Heavenly Father and in the perfect plan of the Son of the Living God, that *all* born-again believers be filled with the Holy Spirit. It is His will, it is His gift, the greatest gift that He could give to the Church.

So you see, when any of the Old Testament prophets were filled with the Spirit, it was a special privilege given to them by God. Today, in this dispensation, it is a gift, a part of God's plan that every member of His Church should be filled with the Holy Spirit.

5. Did Jesus do His healing directly from God or did He do it through the Holy Spirit?

Let me make something very clear to you. God is always the "Big Boss" and has all power in heaven and earth. He is God Almighty and everything comes from Him. He is the mighty Giver, all-powerful, almighty. When Jesus walked upon this earth, He did not do the healing of sick bodies in His own strength. It was the Holy Spirit who did the healing through Him, as I explained more completely in a previous chapter.

I will never forget the day when the Holy Spirit revealed a truth to my heart, because it put a different light on everything. My scriptural basis for the truth of the revelation is in Acts 10:38, for I dare not make any statements without being able to back them up by the Word of God. "God anointed Jesus of Nazareth with the Holy Ghost and with power: who went about doing good, and healing all that were oppressed of the devil; for God was with him."

Here we have all three persons of the Trinity. It was God who gave Jesus the anointing, but it was the power of the Holy Spirit that performed the miracles and did the healing. That's why I go back again to the time when Jesus came up out of the waters of baptism. Remember, Jesus was as much man as though He were not God. He had come in the flesh, literally God in the flesh, but all three persons of the Trinity were present at the baptism of Jesus; and God spoke audibly saying, "This is my beloved Son in whom I am well pleased." At that same moment, the Holy Spirit descended upon Jesus in the form of a dove, equipping Him with power for service. It was the power of the Holy Ghost, the same person who heals today, using the same method then to perform the miracles and do the

137

healings through Jesus Christ the Son. God anointed Jesus with the Holy Ghost.

It is still the Holy Spirit who does the healing today. God sits upon His Throne in heaven, the "Big Boss," the Giver of every gift. At His right hand is seated our great High Priest, our Advocate, the One who ever lives to make intercession for you and for me, Jesus Christ, God's Son. But in that home of yours, in that life of yours, or wherever the Holy Ghost is invited, the same method is used this hour as when Jesus walked this earth. It is the Holy Ghost who does the healing.

6. Did the Gifts of the Holy Spirit cease with the early church? Is it possible to receive gifts of the Holy Spirit today?

My answer to the first part of this question is, "No." My answer to the second part is, "Yes." Any gift that was manifested through the members of the early Church is for Christians today. In the twelfth chapter of First Corinthians, we see there are diversities of gifts and operations of the Spirit; and it is God through the Holy Spirit who gives certain gifts to certain people—given not as they will but as He wills.

If one has really been given one or more of the gifts of the Spirit, that person to whom the gift or gifts have been given will never boast about it. Neither will he advertise it. If you are asking why this is so, it is simply because that one recognizes the fact that it is the Holy Spirit, not the one to whom the gift was given, who manifests His power through a body of flesh. All that you or I can do is furnish the body, the yielded vessel. We furnish no wisdom, no knowledge, no real talent because all of these things are in the natural. All that we give to God is a surrendered vessel, and He uses the temple of clay as His temple, and it is the power of the Holy Spirit who manifests Himself and His own power.

Therefore, that one who has so yielded himself in complete consecration to the Lord to be used of Him, will recognize the fact that God has given him a special gift. *He will not boast of it, however, for among the greatest of Christian graces is humility.* When one is really and truly filled with the Spirit, *he will demonstrate humility.* There will be *no* spiritual pride in that person.

> *The grace of the Lord Jesus Christ, and the love of God, and the communion of the Holy Ghost, be with you all. Amen.*

(2 Corinthians 13:14)

139

Kathryn Kuhlman's words . . .

For Those Who
Need a Miracle

"I believe in miracles with every atom of my being . . . because I believe in God.

Remember, Kathryn Kuhlman has nothing to do with the healing of sick bodies. I have no healing power. It's the power of God that does the healing. The only part I have is making Jesus real to the hearts of men and women.

Jesus is now seated at the right hand of God the Father in the position of our High Priest. Before Jesus went away, He said He would send the Holy Spirit . . . and He came! In the world today is the Holy Spirit. He is the power of the Trinity.

There is no power in the universe that is greater than the power of the Holy Spirit. I am still awed when I see His power in action. Don't ever feel your condition is hopeless. You put that affliction alongside the bigness of God. No person is hopeless; no person need ever be defeated on a single score, as long as God is still on His Throne.

It's His love, His great compassion, His power. Just now in this moment, forget everything else. Take your eyes off of yourself, off of your circumstance. See Him, He is still God Almighty. Do you believe it with all your heart? Do you believe His Word? That's all that Abraham had, but it was sufficient. All that Moses had was God's Word; it was sufficient. YOU have His Word, YOU have His promise in Jeremiah 33:3: "Call unto me, and I will answer thee, and shew thee great and mighty things, which thou knowest not."

Have you ever called? Have you ever asked? Do it just now and I promise you something: He'll hear the cry of your heart. He loves you and He is the answer to your need.

Father God, just now hear that cry . . . and may the glorious power of the Holy Spirit flow through that body, I pray. Give that one the desire of their heart, for Jesus' sake we ask it. And we vow to give you the praise forever and ever. Amen."

142

A Message to the Readers

When reminiscing about the early years of her life, her conversion in that little Methodist Church in Concordia, Missouri, and her call into the ministry, Kathryn Kuhlman stated:

"I was converted at the age of fourteen. My call from Him to preach was as definite as my conversion. I was young and inexperienced. All that I knew was that Jesus had forgiven my sins.

I began preaching in Idaho. You can name any little town in that state, and I evangelized it. I would find any little country church that could not afford a preacher and get permission to hold services in it. The very first sermon I preached was Zaccheus up a tree, and God knows that if anyone was up a tree, I certainly was. After about the sixth sermon I preached, I honestly felt I had exhausted the Bible."

But the Bible had not been exhausted—and down through the years of her earthly ministry, Kathryn Kuhlman preached countless sermons. She was one who loved the Word of God, searched the Scriptures, and relied upon the Holy Spirit as her Teacher and the One who revealed to her heart the deep truths of the Word.

Many of her messages and heart-to-heart talks (often referred to by her as "good, old-fashioned Missouri cornbread") have been put into print over the years by the Kathryn Kuhlman Foundation—and they are available today.

If you would like information on other Kathryn Kuhlman materials (books, audio tapes, videos), contact us at the following address. And please don't hesitate to let us know if there is a burden upon your heart or a need in your life for which you desire prayer. Remember, THERE IS NO LIMIT TO GOD'S POWER . . . and what He has done for others, He will do for you!

Kathryn Kuhlman Foundation
P.O. Box 3
Pittsburgh, PA 15230
Phone: 412-882-2033 Fax: 412-882-7745